DAVID
When Only God's Grace Will Do

DAVID

When Only God's Grace Will Do

NORMAN ARCHER

CHRISTIAN HERALD BOOKS

Chappaqua, New York

TO MARY

Christian Herald, independent, evangelical and interdenominational, is dedicated to publishing wholesome, inspirational and religious books for Christian families. "The books you can trust."

MEMBER OF
EVANGELICAL CHRISTIAN
PUBLISHERS ASSOCIATION

Library of Congress Cataloging in Publication Data

Archer, Norman.
   David, when only God's grace will do.

   1. David, King of Israel. I. Steven, Hugh.
II. Steven, Norma. III. Title.
BS580.D3A74   222'.4'0924   79-55680
ISBN 0-915684-56-X

Contents

Preface		7
1.	The Drag Factor	9
2.	Nobody Loves Me	19
3.	Solving Other People's Problems	29
4.	The Bittersweet Taste of Success	40
5.	When Life Becomes a Tangled Mess	52
6.	How to Handle Grief	61
7.	How to Handle Success	74
8.	How to Handle Disappointment	85
9.	A Matter of Adultery	99
10.	Friends Turn Against You	111
11.	God Didn't Answer My Prayer	124
12.	How to Live—and Die	134

Preface

My wife, Norma, and our daughter Karen were at the airport, waiting for the plane that would take them from Canada to our home in Santa Ana, California. With them were my wife's parents, and as they said their final good-byes, Norma's friend Audrey Renney rushed up breathlessly to press a small package into Norma's hands.

"I know we've said good-bye," said Audrey, "but for some reason I felt I should bring you these tapes. They're by Norman Archer, pastor of Emmanuel Baptist Church in Victoria, and because they were such a help to me, I felt they were too good to keep to myself."

We are not avid tape-listeners, but one night when we retired early, we decided to listen to one of the tapes. We were overwhelmed. We could hardly wait to retire early the next night, and the next. Like Audrey, we felt we could not keep Archer's insights to ourselves; and thus began a two-year project to get the tapes into book form and find a publisher for this radically new view of David's life.

But the life of King David has been eulogized in numerous books, fiction and nonfiction, motion pictures, and children's Sunday school songs. Is another treatment of his story necessary? We believe you will agree it is when you read Norman Archer's analysis of David's life. It is exciting, challenging, and refreshingly different. Mr. Archer strips away David's veneer of veneration to present the real "man after God's own heart." He creatively takes David's life and applies it to contemporary situations until it "lives" for the reader. It is drama in print. You will be drawn back to the book time and again. "That's me," you will say. "I'm just like David. And I, too, can be a man or woman after God's own heart."

We are deeply indebted to Norman Archer, now pastor of First Baptist Church, Calgary, Alberta, for his willingness to let us undertake this project. We also want to thank Christian Herald for publishing what we believe to be a book that will change the lives of its readers. And we especially thank Jocelyn Cameron for her enthusiasm for the project and her willingness to transcribe the tapes and type the final manuscript.

Hugh and Norma Steven

1 The Drag Factor
1 Samuel 16:1-13

In the heart of the English countryside, between London and Oxford, lie the Chiltern Hills, a rolling range of simple beauty. I love those green hills, which, although affected to some extent by urban sprawl, still remind me of the days of my youth. There is nothing more delightful for me than to meander through the little scattered villages that nestle there so cozily and to encounter again the people who have lived there all their lives and who still are willing to pass on to you some of their simple wisdom.

Tucked away in one of those sleepy villages is a tinker who to this day earns his living by making and mending pots and pans. He is proud of his trade and is always eager to explain to any interested visitor the steps in making some cooking utensil or other that he happens to be working on.

"I'm making this here pot for Mrs. Puddephatt what lives in that big house over there. So I get me sheet of metal and lay it on me bench like this. Then I take me ruler and measure it off. Now the secret of this game is to be *dead accurate* when you're doing your measuring."

Then he will pause. You know from experience that there

is about to follow some pearl of country wisdom that will stay with you for life.

"It's a funny thing, you know," he says. "It don't matter how accurate you are, you're bound to be a little bit out."

That tinker is referring in his own quaint fashion to what I call "the drag factor." The drag factor is that small problem or irritation or imperfection that exists in every thing and every situation, from a slight irregularity in a handmade pot to a constant drip from the kitchen faucet to mumps at Thanksgiving, a big pimple on your forehead on the night of a big date, or a broken arm at the beginning of summer vacation. The drag factor is usually small and may from an objective standpoint seem relatively insignificant, but it is something that mars an otherwise beautiful situation.

So it is with the human personality. A person may possess great potential, but the drag factor is that little unknown quantity, that little thing, that can upset one's whole world. It is what others have called the "fly in the ointment" or what Paul called his "thorn in the flesh." It is what we mean when we say, "If only our circumstances were different." It is that accident of birth or circumstance that dwarfs everything else in our relationships. It is the one deep problem that holds us back from becoming the kind of people we desire to be.

As we look into David's life, we see him as a developing, maturing person in relationship to God and others. But one of the important elements to observe about David is the drag factor. Let me suggest three areas in which David struggled with his own particular problem: first, the value placed on his life by his family; second, the value he himself placed on his life; and third, the value placed on his life by God.

Try to imagine David's family. They lived in a modest home. It had to be modest, because as you read between the lines of the Old Testament, you realize that Jesse,

David's father, had no servants. There were eight boys in the family, and the menial work was done by the youngest, David. When David went to visit the king he took gifts, but what kind of gifts? He had a single donkey loaded down with bread, one flask of wine, and a kid from the family's small herd of goats.

Notice also that David's place in the household was probably not a happy one. When Samuel came to anoint one of Jesse's sons as the next king of Israel, seven strapping young men appeared before him. When Samuel asked if that was all his sons, Jesse, with what I take to be a sense of disdain, said, "There remaineth yet the youngest, and, behold, he keepeth the sheep" (1 Sam. 16:11, KJV). It is almost as if he had forgotten he had another son.

We know almost nothing about David's mother, but as the story unfolds, we begin to sense that David's brothers had little love for him. From the record, it would seem to me that David lived in a family that ignored him, did not understand him, and did not sympathize with his dreams. In a word, I believe that David's drag factor was a poor self-image.

As we take a close look at David, we notice he was always the activist, always trying to prove himself, always struggling for acceptance, always trying to buy love, always trying to fill up the vacuum he knew existed within the depths of his heart. Like most of us, David found it difficult to handle not being loved and accepted.

In his book *Come to the Party*, Karl A. Olsson traced the effect of the drag factor in family relationships. His theory was that in every family, there are some children who are "blessed" and some who are "unblessed." The prodigal son is one example used by Olsson. "Give me half the inheritance," said the prodigal, and he left home. One of the interesting facts of the story is that the prodigal was a blessed son. He was so secure in his father's love that he felt free to ask for half the inheritance. He was also free to ignore his upbringing and waste his substance with riotous living in a far-off land. He was free to do that because he was the blessed son.

The other son, the older brother, stayed at home. He appears to have been the unblessed son, not free to do anything. Unconsciously, he knew it did not matter how early he got up to perform his chores, how late he went to bed after having worked his fingers to the bone, or how industriously or conscientiously he performed the tasks assigned to him. He knew he could never earn his father's favor. The result was a son who grew up insecure, self-hating, unblessed, and without the freedom to ask anything of his father — certainly not half the inheritance, or even a kid to make merry with his friends.

Most parents are conscious of the importance of fair play in bringing up their children. They know they cannot play favorites. So if they give one piano lessons, they will pay for skating lessons for another. At meal time, one child's juice glass has to contain precisely the same quantity as the other's if a feud is to be avoided. Every detail of family life has to be carefully evaluated to ensure that each child receives his equal portion from the family resources. Yet in spite of our careful efforts to provide equal treatment, we still rear prodigal sons and older brothers, blessed and unblessed children. Look at Joseph's parading around in his coat of many colors, utterly secure and confident in his father's love. Even when he was in prison, Joseph was optimistic. He knew he was the blessed son.

Just what is this blessed son relationship? It is a nonverbal mystery, a particular rapport or nearness established in a family. Once this rapport is assured, the child is free from the anxiety of seeking acceptance. But the unblessed child remains in a constant bondage of unfulfillment.

Abraham was a man of great faith, but only because he knew he was loved by God. Therefore, with that security and confidence, Abraham could deal with Lot, his neighbors, and his family from a position of strength.

In contrast to Abraham, we come to a man like David, the runt of the family who appears to have been completely unblessed. In this book we will see how that status influenced David's interpersonal relationships. We will also study the many interesting people who came into David's life. With some, David had great ability to communicate; with others, his tongue seemed to be tied.

When I was preparing this book, I thought about my own relationship with my brother. I have one brother who is nine years older than I, and it seems to me that he was the blessed son and I was the unblessed. I cannot fault my parents; they were fair and honest, and I have much to be thankful for. But it seemed to me that he could get away with things I could not. That left us not only with a normal sibling rivalry; but I also schemed to discredit my brother. It is far easier to rub another person's crown in the dirt than it is to rise to his level.

And now I am married, with a family of my own. I pride myself on the fair and honest way in which I treat my children and the open way in which we can communicate. I once started a discussion around our meal table about this whole question of being blessed and unblessed, and I asked the various family members if they thought there was one son who was blessed above the others. With one voice they chorused, "Yes!" and pointed to the same one. And I had to admit it was true: I have an especially close relationship with one of my sons. I try to be fair and equal in my dealings with all my children, yet, almost mysteriously, this special rapport developed with one member of the family — I cannot help it or pretend it is not true. I believe, therefore, that one must accept it and deal with it openly and honestly. The same would be true if one of my children were "unblessed."

It is my opinion that David was in the unfortunate predicament of being the unblessed son. That led to the second part of his low self-esteem, the low value he himself placed on his life. It is fascinating to read the psalms and see how they express the turmoil of David's heart. An example is Psalm 51, David's psalm of confession and repentance. In verse 5 he said, "Behold, I was shapen in iniquity; and in sin did my mother conceive me" (KJV). What gave him that idea? Who told him that? Where did he learn that he was shaped in iniquity and conceived in sin? Was it something he had heard as a child? Is it not significant that David did not say, "We were *all* shaped in iniquity"?

Commentary writers and other theologians have waxed eloquent on this verse and used it to demonstrate the reality of original sin. I do not dispute that position, but I think there is far more in this verse than most theologians have considered. David was not trying to be theological or attempting to expound a doctrine. Rather, he was crying from the depths of his own being — that was how he felt. Notice also Psalm 27:10: "When my father and my mother forsake me" (KJV). Why did David talk like that unless he had literally experienced the pain of being forsaken?

Then came the experience in Psalm 38:1-4 when David said: "O Lord, rebuke me not in thy wrath: neither chasten me in thy hot displeasure. For thine arrows stick fast in me, and thy hand presseth me sore. There is no soundness in my flesh because of thine anger; neither is there any rest in my bones because of my sin. For mine iniquities are gone over mine head: as an heavy burden they are too heavy for me" (KJV).

Psalm 25:7 may give us a further insight into David's personality. "Remember not the sins of my youth," he said. Here is a grown man, king of Israel, talking about the sins of his youth. Why? It seems that his boyhood guilt hung over him like a dark shadow—he had never known real forgiveness.

A university student once came to me and told me she

had been brought up in a Christian home. She said her parents were godly, and she had become a Christian as a young child. Then the young woman told me her problem. "I can't really be sure that God has forgiven me," she said. "Again and again in my prayers I say, 'Lord forgive me, I confess my sin.' I remind myself that Christ has come into my life to be my Savior. I claim all those promises, but somehow deep down, I can't really feel free from my sin."

We talked for a while and in the course of the conversation got around to family backgrounds. Little by little, pieces of the puzzle began to fit together, and I discovered a girl who never really knew forgiveness. She would do something wrong, be found out, and say, "I'm sorry." Mom or Dad would say, "I forgive you," but they never let her forget her sin. Week after week, month after month, it was brought up time and again. Therefore, when somebody said, "God has forgiven you," the only thing she could hear was God saying, "Very well, you are forgiven, but I won't let you forget it. I'll be reminding you periodically of your sin."

David was in that situation. The sins of his youth dogged his footsteps and made him wretched and miserable inside, thus destroying his sense of self-worth.

Now let's see the other side of the picture, the value God placed on his life. This is the key to the whole mystery. One of the fascinating ways God deals with us is through His ability to make good come out of the raw materials we place in His hands. When we give Him water, He turns it into wine. When we give to Him the wrath of man, He makes it result in praise to Him. It staggers my mind to realize that God is able to take man at his worst, when he is the most unlovely, when he vents his wrath, and not just remove that wrath but also cause it to bring Him praise. The miracle is that God makes something good that would never have been there at all if it had not been for the wrath of man.

Here, then, is David, the unblessed man, with the large drag factor looming in his life, who finally puts his unblessed life into God's hands. What did God do? Did God suddenly change it all and make David a blessed man? Certainly not. Many Christians think that once they become Christians and are new creations, they are going to be different people. But that is not the way God works. God takes those very characteristics that were produced because of an unblessed situation and refines them. He does not remove those warped and twisted parts of our personalities. Rather, He refines them and makes them tools to accomplish good. He did with David what He never could have done had David been a blessed son. David kept going to God with all his unfulfilled wants until finally he woke up and said, "The Lord is my Shepherd, I shall not want." David still had to work out of the experience of his home environment. But because he had entered into a new relationship with God, he had a new sense of acceptance.

David's psalms vibrate with the theme of a person with inhibitions, fears, frustrations, and self-rejection. Yet he was able to say, "Rest in the LORD, and wait patiently for him" (Psalm 37:7a, KJV). He turned to God in Psalm 17:8 and said without fear of rejection, "Keep me as the apple of your eye." In Psalm 16:8 and 11 he said, "I have set the LORD always before me, . . . I shall not be moved. . . . Thou wilt shew me the path of life: in thy presence is fullness of joy; at thy right hand there are pleasures for evermore" (KJV).

David discovered that once he put his drag factor in God's hand, it became a thrust-factor. It is not that God uses us in spite of the things that plague us. Rather, He uses us *because* of them. It is not that we rise above them and manage to keep our heads above water because God is underneath, pushing us up from the bottom. Rather, God says, "Because you are in that situation, I can make far more out of you than I could if you had never been there. It is because you are down low that I can lift you up higher."

My impossibility becomes His possibility. My weakness becomes His strength.

Second Corinthians is a book that shows us how much Paul believed this truth. The church at Corinth wanted to make Paul into a great person. There were a great many self-styled apostles going around who were doing miracles and giving glowing testimonies, and the Corinthians wanted Paul to do the same. "If you're going to be a leader, we want to see great things coming from you," they said as they sat back and waited for Paul's glowing testimony. But Paul said, in essence, "If you want to remember me, remember me as a frightened little man who crouched inside a basket and was let down the side of a wall and ran for his life. This is how I deserve to be remembered — in all my weakness, in all my failure, in all my fear."

We Christians have too long believed that the way to make the gospel effective in our world is to produce "Super-Christians." We have been told to look victorious, to keep a smile on our faces, to square our shoulders, to show how great God is — with us, in us, and through us — how adequate we become because of Him. But Paul never did that. His approach was to bring his inner problems and incompleteness, his drag factors, into his teaching of the gospel.

David's approach was the same. He said, "Bring your fears, your failures, your sins, and your doubts into your relating of divine experience to others." That is what the book of Psalms is all about. If we hide our weakness, we will also hide Christ. We will no longer present a real Jesus. Under those circumstances our Lord becomes cold, harsh, impersonal, and an unreal, stained-glass-window characterization who meets no one's needs or aspirations. But God is real! Therefore Paul was able to say, "Of course I will glory in my weakness — it is my opportunity to demonstrate Christ's great strength" (2 Cor. 12:9, author's paraphrase).

We need to live and witness honestly so that onlookers will see Christ at work in the brokenness of our circumstances. At times we see only the unsolved problems, and we are afraid that they are all other people will see, too. The only thing Paul could see in Romans 7 was his "thorn in the flesh," his drag factor. But as onlookers with the perspective of history, we see Christ glorified in that weak vessel. Frequently, all David could see was the pain of his humanity as he said, "Against Thee only have I sinned and done this evil in thy sight," or "I am weak O Lord," or "I am weary with my groanings." But again, with the perspective of time, we do not see a weakling. We see a man after God's own heart.

What is your drag factor? What is it that makes you, like the tinker's pot, "a little bit out"? What is it that mars your life and holds you back? What is it that makes you hobble through life? Most of us think we would love to be different or freed from a handicap. But the challenge of Scripture is that we take our drag factors, whatever they are, put them into God's hand, and watch Him make them into thrust-factors — not for our glory, but for His.

Discussion Questions

1. Do you agree that David was the "unblessed son" and had a poor self-image? Why or why not?
2. What truths or examples are there in David's life that can help us understand and cope with poor self-image?
3. Are there blessed and unblessed children in your family? Is it possible or necessary for parents to feel the same about each child?
4. Can you think of experiences in your life when God brought about a good result for His glory because of your weaknesses?

2 Nobody Loves Me
1 Samuel 17:12-16, 24-30

A fire once swept through a great building and in a few hours reduced it to ashes. What is interesting is that the building contained several thousand tons of ice. Later a newspaper reporter wrote, "Although the building contained thousands of gallons of potential extinguisher, it was not in an available form." Its assets were frozen!

Many churches suffer from this same disorder. They have within their fellowships enormous potential in God-given abilities. Yet that potential frequently remains hidden, never developed or utilized. Consequently those "frozen assets" do nothing for the local body of believers or for the extension of Christ and His Kingdom.

Part of the reason Scripture calls us to growth and maturity in Christ is to enrich our lives and bring to light our special gifts, those frozen assets, that God has put within us to benefit His church. Locked within our lives are experiences, abilities, and qualities that can be used greatly by the Holy Spirit. Yet many people feel they are so hampered, so limited, that they seldom reach the potential for which God designed them. Others, entangled with psychological problems, are shy and nervous, eaten up with anxiety and fear. They think they cannot possibly break through to do anything worthwhile for Christ's sake. Some who feel they have been victimized in some way and are emotionally scarred may sing the same dirge.

But let's scrutinize the things we call our liabilities. We may discover they are our assets. They may be frozen assets — locked up — but assets nonetheless, and in God's hands they can be thawed and brought to the surface to be of blessing and encouragement to the church body.

As we examine David's life, we discover that he suffered incredible limitations. It seems likely that David's home background left him with deep emotional scars, and in 1 Samuel 17:12-16, 24-30, we find yet another of David's problems. David's oldest brothers had enlisted in the army to fight the Philistines. David, dispatched by his father, was to take supplies to his brothers. When he arrived, he saw this great giant, Goliath of Gath, challenging the armies of Israel. David began to ask what was going on. In his probing, David ran into his oldest brother, Eliab. And from the remarks in verse 28, we discover that Eliab was far from happy to see his younger brother.

I suggest that that was no isolated incident. I suggest that David and Eliab were always at odds with each other and that David was criticized and rejected not only on this particular occasion but on many other occasions as well. Even in this same chapter, when David offered his service to King Saul, Saul said, "Don't be ridiculous! How can a boy like you fight with a man like him?" This kind of rejection happened many times, and it had its effect on David's self-image.

My thesis is that because of his rejection and poor self-image, David was starved for love. And to make matters worse, love was the one thing he could not handle. Put David in front of a Philistine and he knew what to do.

Put him at the head of an army and he could fight. Put him on the throne and he could rule like few others. But give David love and he did not know what to do with it. He would get embarrassed and frustrated and do the most incredible, outrageous things. David never knew how to handle love.

I believe we see this in David's relationship with Jonathan. I further believe that it was a one-sided relationship, because the Bible never says David loved Jonathan. What you do find in the Bible is that Jonathan loved David. It comes out time and again. But David, it seems, could not return Jonathan's love. He did not know what to do with it. When David learned that Jonathan had been killed in battle, David launched out in a beautiful lament, talking about his relationship with Jonathan: "I am distressed for thee, my brother Jonathan: very pleasant hast thou been unto me: thy love to me was wonderful, passing the love of women" (2 Sam. 1:26, KJV). But there was no mention of any love for Jonathan.

True, David developed a relationship with Bathsheba, but it was an immoral kind of love built more on getting than on giving. David developed a relationship based on infatuation with Michal, King Saul's daughter, whom he later married. Yet there is never a hint that David loved Michal. You do find, however, several references to Michal's love for David. And the love David developed for his sons Absalom and Solomon was an indulgent kind of love, and both sons suffered because of it.

Remarkably, David's psalms contain few references to love. From a concordance study, I found that when David said he loved, the object of his love was almost always some thing or some place, not some person. David loved things and places and qualities in people, but you do not find him saying he loved anybody. Only twice did David hint that he even loved the Lord. In Psalm 31:23, David, standing on a soapbox, preaching a sermon, told other people to love God. In effect he said, "Don't do what I am doing; do what I am telling you to do."

However, there were many occasions when David said he hated. Perhaps at this point you are casting about in your mind for a psalm that will disprove my theory. I will forestall you. Psalm 116:1 says, "I love the LORD, because he hath heard my voice" (KJV). But David did not write Psalm 116. There are several psalms that say "I love the Lord," but in most cases they are not David's psalms. Love and David had problems — they did not mix.

As far as David was concerned, love was virtually a meaningless word. He had received so little of it as a child that he never knew how to give it as an adult. What was the impact of this upon his life?

What David truly wanted in life (the psalms giving us insight into David's deepest desires) was to be at one with someone and to have that someone be at one with him. I detect a profound loneliness in David. Perhaps the closest he ever got to achieving this oneness was in his relationship with Jonathan. David spent most of his life trying to overcome this sense of isolation and loneliness. He tried to overcome it with Saul, but that relationship did not work out. He tried with his brothers but found he had to defend himself. "I know what kind of a cocky brat you are," said Eliab. "You just want to see the battle!" He tried with Jonathan, but he could not return the love Jonathan gave him. He tried with one wife and then with another. And when he failed in interpersonal relationships, David tried to achieve satisfaction through popularity, accomplishments, and military victories.

The interesting thing is that many of us do the same thing. We are lonely, isolated people, with aching hearts, trying to overcome our sense of separation. There is separation even within families, separation we first feel as children. Later, when we grow up and leave home, still feeling emotionally hungry and dissatisfied, we launch into marriage, believing it will satisfy the deep hunger. And one day we discover that our wives or husbands cannot or do not satisfy that need. We make friendships with the hope of enriching our lives, but, alas, we discover that our friends are human after all, with their own problems and limitations. And then we do what David did. We get involved with organizations and with the public to sink ourselves into some kind of institutional relationship. Many lonely people living in an impersonal society come into a church for that very purpose — to try to find warmth, comfort, and security.

Although David was himself vulnerable and sensitive, he showed little concern for the feelings of others. He was a man who manipulated and schemed. Indirectly, this drive for power destroyed his son Absalom. Absalom grew up in this power-struggle environment, rebelled against his father, and ultimately was killed. It destroyed Solomon, his other son who was always overindulged. When Solomon became king, he was unprepared and unfit for government. His unsuitability to assume the throne resulted after his death in the division of the kingdom and a rift in the nation that would never heal.

David was a casualty similar to the young man Otto Will, Jr., wrote about who came from a "good" family,

[who] knows the aloneness and the growing terror, the living in a world peopled by those who listen but do not hear, who speak but do not communicate, who demand affection but do not give tenderness, who invite closeness and cannot tolerate intimacy, who smile and frown and sneer and laugh in a fashion perpetually and hopelessly inappropriate, who insist that they love but do not notice the pain of the loved one, who encourage the accomplishment of the impossible, who proclaim that there is hope while their own lives so clearly act out despair. He knows all this so well that he has come to live

on the alert, expecting to find in all humans that destruc-
tiveness which he found in a few [Otto Allen Will, Jr.,
quoted in Reuel Howe, *Man's Need and God's Action* (Clin-
ton, Mass.: Seabury, 1953), pp. 37-38].

But happily, there was fruit that came out of David's
liabilities. First let me say that if you think I am being hard
on David or unjustly critical of him, I confess that I might
be; but I think that is because I hate pedestals. Frequently
we make Bible characters unreal and unreachable. The
Bible never does that. I'm glad! I cannot relate to pedestals,
but I can relate to real people.

Let me tell you a little bit about myself. There is nobody
more surprised than I when people show up each Sunday
at the church I pastor. Sometimes I lie awake on a Saturday
night, tossing and turning, saying to myself, *Suppose nobody comes*. Occasionally I visit other churches and sit under
the ministry of another preacher, and when I leave I ask
myself, *Why do people come to hear* me *preach?* I look through
my sermons and they seem so thin. Yet Sunday comes
along, and so do people. And I say, "Thank You, Lord; You
have given me another chance!" But even my thanksgiving
is short-lived, because immediately my mind is flooded
with Milton's line: "The hungry sheep look up and are not
fed." When I confess my feelings, I know somebody will
say, "Ah, but you should get the victory over that! You
don't have a very spiritual attitude!" And they are right. So
I wrestle with the Lord and say, "Well, it's not me they've
come to hear anyway. They've come to worship God." And
for about five minutes I feel better.

Then another voice takes over and says, "Who do you
think you are, anyway? Do you think God will use you?
Look at all the books you've read about God's using only
clean vessels and sanctified lives. Look at all those biographies you've read about a person whose life was fully
surrendered and utterly committed. People only had to

meet them and their lives were blessed. But look at you with your prickly personality. See how quickly you get irritated and cross and how preoccupied you are with yourself. How much does your congregation know about what's going on in your mind? How do you ever expect God to use a person like you?"

In the middle of this I begin to think about good old David — a man who made such a mess of so many things. Almost all his human relationships were chaotic. He irritated his brothers. His father would apparently rather forget him and keep him out with the sheep. It was as if David had an invisible label over his head: "Not to be introduced to visitors." David irritated Saul so much that Saul threw a dagger at him. He also irritated his wife Michal so much that we read that she "despised him in her heart." He irritated his son Absalom so much that teenage rebellion became open revolution. And so it went, on and on and on.

Perhaps one reason I like David is that I so easily identify with him. Nobody was more surprised than David when people applauded him. "Saul has killed his thousands and David his tens of thousands!" Nobody was more surprised than David that Jonathan loved him, loved him with the kind of love he did not or could not return. Read 1 Samuel 18. David did not feel worthy of that kind of attention. He did not feel worthy to have King Saul be interested in him. He felt unworthy to marry the king's daughter: "Who am I? and what is my life or my father's family in Israel, that I should be son-in-law to the king?" (1 Sam. 18:18, KJV). When talking to the messengers in verse 23 of the same chapter, David said to Saul's servants, "Seemeth it to you a light thing to be a king's son-in-law, seeing that I am a poor man, and lightly esteemed?" (KJV).

Then, when David was about to marry that first daughter of King Saul in verse 19, she was given to another. That was

what always happened to David. There was always someone around the corner better than he was, someone whose
personality was sweeter, whose mature characteristics
were more attractive, and it was such a man who married
Saul's first daughter.

David could easily have said, "God, why me? Why not
Jonathan? He is ten times the man that I am. Why did
Samuel anoint me to be king? You know what kind of a
person I am."

Suppose for a moment that it *was* Jonathan who was
anointed king instead of David. Do you know how the
Bible record would have read then? "Jonathan did that
which was right in the sight of the Lord, and the Lord
prospered him. The end." That would have been it. Time
and again you find that kind of person appearing on the
pages of the Old Testament, and the Bible says very little
more about them.

Do you realize what we would have lost had Jonathan or
someone as worthy as Jonathan been king in the place of
David? We would have lost such things as the passion of
Psalm 6:6-7: "I am weary with my groaning...I water my
couch with tears.... Mine eye is consumed because of
grief" (KJV). We would have lost Psalm 22:1: "My God, my
God, why hast thou forsaken me?" (KJV). And we would
not have the heart-yearning of David in Psalm 24:3-5:
"Who shall ascend into the hill of the LORD? Or who shall
stand in his holy place? He that hath clean hands and a pure
heart; who hath not lifted up his soul unto vanity, nor
sworn deceitfully. He shall receive the blessing" (KJV). And
a great loss would be Psalm 23:1-3: "The Lord is my
shepherd; I shall not want. He maketh me to lie down in
green pastures.... He restoreth my soul" (KJV).

Suppose David had been the blessed son, secure and
emotionally mature, with no harmful inhibitions or interpersonal problems. He would have been a great king, and

that would be that. But it is because he was weak and so unlikely a candidate that our hearts are warmed toward him, as in Psalm 51:1-3 when he cried out, "Have mercy upon me, O God, according to thy lovingkindness: according unto the multitude of thy tender mercies blot out my transgressions. Wash me thoroughly from mine iniquity, and cleanse me from my sin. For I acknowledge my transgressions: and my sin is ever before me" (KJV).

David was not fooled by all the congratulations that came his way. Nor was he fooled by all his apparent success. He knew himself, and he knew the greatness of his God. Those were David's frozen assets. Until they were touched by God, they were liabilities. But when they were warmed and thawed by God, they became the means whereby the wonder and power of God were manifested.

Ole Bull, the great violinist of a bygone age, once gave a concert in Paris. Just as the concert began, his A string broke. A lesser man would have stopped, but Ole Bull went on to play the entire concert on three strings. Ole Bull lived long before my time, but if I had been given one opportunity to hear him play, I would have chosen the concert played on three strings.

When God takes a man with a broken A string and makes beautiful music, that's grace. And that is David's kind of God. Many years later, another man who knew something of the weight of physical limitations and the encumbrances of liabilities wrote in 2 Corinthians 12:10b: "For when I am weak, then I am strong — the less I have, the more I depend on him."

Discussion Questions

1. Do you agree that David did not know how to love, not even God? Why or why not? If he was becoming progressively more a man after God's own heart, why did he not grow in his ability to love?
2. What are your liabilities that keep your assets frozen?
3. What other biblical personalities can you think of whom God brought to maturity through difficult circumstances and in spite of handicaps? What personal acquaintances of your own can you think of?
4. What talents are going unused in your church?

3 Solving Other People's Problems
1 Samuel 17:32-50

If we could find a person who was completely psychologically healthy, emotionally mature, and spiritually secure, he would probably be able to laugh at himself. I can sometimes smile at myself, but I have not arrived at the point of being able to have a good "belly laugh" at my own expense. But I know that when you can laugh at your situation, your circumstances, and your profession, you are indeed maturing. And although I cannot quite laugh at myself, I can laugh at my profession. There is no breed quite so comical as preachers.

Several years ago I read a delightful article called "Clergy Birds" that exemplifies what I mean about being able to laugh at yourself. Part of it reads as follows:

Last year devoted groups of lovers of "clergy birds" banded themselves together to form the National Association for Clergy Bird Classification and Preservation — the N.A.C.C.P. Equally important to the work of the new society is the classification of clergy birds. Some of the rarest and most unusual birds in America are to be found among this species. To date, the following have been observed: the two-year church switcher; the limp-limbed handgripper; the ivory-tufted hale fellow; the double-chinned diet dodger; the Scot mimic-brogue; the smooth-talking say nothing; the Fosdick sermon swiper; the broad-smiling compromiser; the velvet-robed pomp; the quick-nodding note watcher; the wide-eyed member counter; the yellow-bellied knuckle-under; the preying member snitcher; the strong-minded people pusher; the swift-adding money minder; the rosy do-gooder; the broad-tailed office percher; the white-collared book bragger; the long-faced killjoy; the full-breasted bull shooter; the chicken-livered issue dodger; the purple-throated pulpit pounder; the scarlet-crested riot reader; and the speckled deacon sniper.

The article continued and told about clergy bird nesting habits, migratory habits, and the best time to observe them in their best plumage — Sundays, of course.

I welcome this kind of input, because when we are able to laugh at ourselves, we are freed from burdensome concerns about image and are able to relax and see ourselves as we really are, not as we piously pretend to be. One reason I love the Bible is that it gives us this kind of input. Scripture is so real, so beautifully honest, so utterly, almost simplistically, transparent. Whenever we see a character in Scripture, we learn about his total humanity, the good and the bad. But then we often invest the same character with unreality. We dress him up and put him in stained-glass windows; sometimes we even give him a halo! Yet a close examination of Scripture reveals all those characters to be made of ordinary human clay.

David was such a man. But Christendom has sometimes encased David in a veneer that God never intended him to have. I believe the folklore that has grown around the story of David and Goliath is a case in point. Let's take a fresh look at the account of David and Goliath. We want to watch David grow in maturity and see what God can do with a person who began his life deprived, unloved, and with little apparent potential.

First, let's check David's motives for enlisting. To begin, I ask a question of myself. Why am I a preacher? What were my motives for entering the ministry? The reaction most people expect is, "Because God called me." And that is true, but no minister has totally pure motives. No one does. All of us have psychological needs that must be met. God recognizes our mixed motives. He recognizes our needs, and He recognizes that we do things for reasons other than those we tell our friends — and He capitalizes on those mixed motives.

All of us, including pastors, need to be needed. This is one reason many ministers find it almost impossible to retire. The reason they often give is that the Lord's work is never done, and that, of course, is true. But that is not the only reason. I suspect that beneath the surface are all kinds of lesser motives, such as the need to be needed. It is hard for us to think we are not needed. Most of us can identify with the self-sacrificing mother who on some occasion may be ill yet who insists on getting up and cooking breakfast for her family. Sometimes she will even drag herself around for the rest of the day to sweep, dust, polish, and clean. If you ask her why, she will say, "Well, it's my job. I can't fail my family; they need me!" They do indeed need her, but it is also true that *she* needs *them*, and she cannot bear to think that they might be able to manage without her.

Now, what has this to do with David and Goliath? In 1 Samuel 17:17, David was given a specific job to do. One day Jesse, David's father, said to David, "Take this bushel of roasted grain and ten loaves of bread to your brothers. Give this cheese to their captain, see how the boys are getting along, and bring back a letter from them" (author's paraphrase).

Those were clear, unambiguous instructions. They left no room for doubt in David's mind about what was expected of him. But what happened? Verse 23 tells us that as he was talking with some of the Israeli soldiers, he saw the giant Goliath step out of the Philistine troops and shout his challenge to the army of Israel. As soon as they saw him, the Israeli soldiers ran in fright. David, curious, asked who this Goliath was. He talked to a few others and then asked, "What will a man get for killing this Philistine and ending his insults to Israel?" (1 Sam. 17:26).

When David's oldest brother, Eliab, heard David (v. 28), he was angry. "What are you doing around here, anyway?" he said. "What about the sheep you're supposed to be taking care of? I know what a cocky brat you are; you just want to see the battle!"

"What have I done now?" David replied (v. 29). "I was only asking a question!"

Now here is the most important point. When he took stock of the problem, David said to the king, "Don't worry about a thing.... I'll take care of this Philistine!" (v. 32). Goliath was a great problem to the Israeli army and to the entire nation, yet David said, "Leave it to me; I'll deal with it." I suggest that Goliath was not David's problem, and David should not have got involved in it. The instructions from his father were explicit and did not include enmeshing himself with the army or entangling himself with Goliath. And you can search the Scriptures from one end to the other and never find any indication that God called David to deal with this problem.

You may say to me, "Yes, but the *need* was the call. You have to deal with a need when you see it. You don't wait for a special call." But I suggest that such an attitude leads to the problem of fighting spiritual battles with human resources. When a person moves in and says, "Leave it to me; I'll do it," what is he trying to prove? What was David trying to prove? He was trying to establish the notion that he was needed. He had a need to be needed. "But it worked, didn't it?" I can hear somebody say. Yes, David did the job and solved the problem. But do you suppose God had no means other than David to deal with the Goliath problem?

When we jump in quickly and say, "Leave the problem to me," we try to make ourselves indispensable to God. Because the need is there, we feel we must meet it. In essence we say, "See how important I am to You, God?"

For those who object and think they never have these feelings, I have a question. Why do so many people insist on carrying loads of responsibility that are too heavy, loads that corrode one's family life? God does not give us more than we can carry. God gives us strength and just enough to meet the responsibilities He wants us to take. It is only when we think we must solve somebody else's problem that we start to wilt under the strain.

David, however, was convinced he was doing the Lord's will. But I wonder how pure his motives really were. After all, David had his own mountain of problems. Have you noticed that sometimes it is easier to solve other people's problems than it is to solve your own? Oh yes, I know there are occasions when the end seems to justify the means. But that does not prove David was doing the right thing. All it proves is that God is a God of incredible grace. We rush in and God blesses — that is amazing grace. We are not called, but God blesses. Sometimes we even create greater problems by our interfering, yet God still blesses.

It is at this point that I take heart. I love David; he is my hero — not because he went around killing giants with slingshots, but because he was a person like me who blundered along, irritating some people, annoying his family, and trying to prove something. Yet God did not laugh, give him up, or leave him to fall flat on his face. God said, "All

right, David, if that's the way you want it, I won't let you
fall. I'm not going to desert you. If you want to get involved
in this problem, which is really none of your business, if
you want to get involved in this thing to which I have not
appointed you, then I'll let you solve it, and I'll let you get
the praise and the smiles of approval and the acceptance
you're so hungry for." God did it for David, and He has also
done it for me and probably you, too.

Let's go on a bit further now and examine David's
methods. David was bent on solving this Goliath problem
for the nation, but the question comes next, how was he
going to do it? In every situation in which there is a decision
to be made, two considerations become prominent for the
decision-maker: first, what is best for me; and second,
what is best for others? Out of these alternatives, he may
sometimes choose the first and do what is best for himself.
Sometimes he may choose the second and do what is best
for others. And on rare occasions, his choice may turn out
to be the best for both parties.

David had several alternatives with which to solve the
Goliath problem. First, David could have dealt with the
Goliath problem by killing him. That is the direction he
chose to go, and it solved Israel's problem. It may have
been the best alternative for Israel, but I do not think it was
the best for Goliath, and I also do not think it was the best
for David. Why, then, did David choose that method?
Because the only way David knew how to deal with problems was to kill them. And that attitude was a result of his
background.

What does an unwanted, unloved child do when he is
stuck out in the hills? He learns to fight and keep on
fighting, because he knows that if he ever quits fighting he
may die. And if he cannot win by direct confrontation, he
will invent new techniques — subtle, crafty things — and
do anything, as long as he wins. Generally, however,

David dealt with his problems by killing them — the lion, the bear, and even Goliath. It was the only method he knew.

But I believe there was another alternative, another way David could have solved the Goliath problem, an alternative that never entered David's head. David could have loved Goliath. Abraham Lincoln had the right idea when he said, "The best way to destroy your enemies is to make them your friends." You might say, "It is unlikely that Goliath could ever be won by love to become a friend of the Israelites." And I would say, "It's no more unlikely than that a shepherd boy could kill an armed giant with a pebble." If David had won Goliath over with love, Israel's problem would have been solved just as effectively. It would also have been the best for Goliath and the best for David. Then why didn't David take that approach? The answer is that David could not love. "Love" was not in his vocabulary.

But David knew how to hate, and what does God do in such circumstances? He uses what we have — our imperfect, often troubled personalities — and makes the wrath of man to praise Him. God even uses the wrong things we put in His hands. I cannot count the number of times that I have given bad advice and taken the wrong approach in counseling situations, nor can I count the number of times that in leading my church I have sent the people in wrong directions and encouraged them to make wrong moves. A professor once said to me, "During the first five years of my ministry, I suppose I preached every heresy that has ever vexed the Christian church." And I can almost say the same thing.

But the astounding thing to me is that somehow it all worked out right. God took the errors, the sins, the blunders, and the poor judgment and made good come out of them. That is amazing grace. The good that has come out of my errors has often been good in the lives of others rather than in my life. I have had Goliath-sized problems to deal with, for example, and I have tackled them without realizing that there was more than one way to deal with them. But by the grace of God things have worked out well for the people with the problems, even though the results have not always been to my best advantage.

I would like to suggest, then, that if David had chosen the better way, he, too, would have benefited. This applies to our personal lives as well. It applies to our families. Frequently our children have Goliath-like problems to deal with, and because we are aware of our human weaknesses, we pray for wisdom and guidance. Yet when we sit down to deal with the problems, we seem to be all on our own. We struggle over the question of what is the best decision, and because our sense of responsibility is heavy, we tackle the problems ourselves and solve them. But we do not always solve them the best way.

When Paul wrote his first letter to the Corinthians, he wrote to a church with horrendous problems. By the time Paul came to the end of chapter 12, he had given the Corinthian church so many bits of advice that their heads were beginning to whirl. Read First Corinthians and try to do the things Paul tells us to do. You will find it to be incredibly difficult. But at the end of chapter 12, after giving many important instructions, Paul in effect said, "Oh, forget it, forget it! I want to show you a more excellent way; here's the real way to deal with it." And then he launched into the beautiful thirteenth chapter, the chapter of love.

After deciding he would tackle the problem, David had to decide how to accomplish it. First he had an encounter with King Saul. Saul, of course, could not think of anyone's going into battle without armor, so he gave David his helmet of brass, his coat of mail, and his sword. But David rejected Saul's armor. Why? Couldn't God use David if he were dressed in Saul's armor? Of course He could have used him. If David had decided to wear Saul's armor and go clunking out to meet Goliath, God would have found a way to overcome David's silliness and accomplish His purpose. But David's rejection of Saul's armor meant only that David chose to use the weapons with which he was familiar, slingshot and stones.

When God called Moses, He said, "Moses, I want you to be the leader of My people."

And Moses said, "But I don't have the equipment. I don't have the wherewithal. I stammer and stutter."

God simply said, "Moses, what do you have? I'm not interested in what you don't have. Tell me what you do have!"

"But I only have a shepherd's rod and a staff in my hand!"

"Very well," said God. "I'll use them."

When the hungry multitude came to Jesus, the disciples said, "How are we going to feed all these people?"

Jesus did not say, "Well, I'm going to give you what you don't have." He said, "What do you have?"

"Some small bread rolls and a few fish."

"Good," said Jesus. "Bring them. I'll use them."

When Jesus was at a wedding and the host ran out of wine, Jesus' mother came to Him for help. "What do you have?" said Jesus.

"Only water," came the reply.

"Good," said Jesus. "I'll use water and make it into wine."

In Sunday school we learned that David was a brave but weak little boy with only five pebbles who challenged the greatest soldier on earth. I do not agree with that version of the story. There is an old soldier's saying that goes, "God is on the side of the army with the best artillery." Although that is a bit cynical, the fact remains that David possessed a powerful weapon. He was not just a tiny boy with five little stones. He knew the power and effectiveness of a hurling stone, and he knew he could use them. But why five stones? If he was such an accurate shot, why not just one stone? Some people would have looked at Goliath and said, "He's so big, how can I win?" David looked at Goliath and said, "He's so big, how can I miss?" But I also agree with John Hercus, who said in his book *David* (Chicago: InterVarsity, 1968) that the choosing of five stones allows us to see another side of David, the maturing side. This wild, savage lad showed a side that only God could see — humility. No one would have suspected it at that point, but when David picked up the five stones, he in effect turned to God and said, "God, You've helped me kill bears and lions, but this is a new problem. I've never seen a giant before. I don't know what kind of skull he's got. He's so big I can't miss, but suppose my first shot doesn't stop him. I've got four more, but if I don't bring him down in five, I'll have no more time." That was true humility. False humility would say, "O God, I'm no good at this." True humility says, "God, I'm the champion, but I'm *only* a champion."

Sometimes we put God into a small circle. We put tools into His hands and He uses them, and we build our theology on it. Then we say, "Look, look, we've proved this is what God uses. We've proved this is God's way. God has blessed it. We've proved this is the right way, the right thing!" No, you have not proved any such thing. All you have proved is that the grace of God works. All of us should understand that it is pure grace when God does *anything* in us or through us.

Take a closer look at Jesus Christ on the cross, and see how wide His arms are extended. That is the width of His grace. When Christ died upon the cross, His arms were extended so wide that He did not lay down conditions or make stipulations beyond faith, nor did He tie Himself down to a prescribed way of using us. He said, "Come just as you are. Come with all your wrong decisions, your mistakes, all your phoniness, and everything else about you. And if that is all you are, that is what I will take and that is what I will use." Jesus accepts us with all our blunderings, with all our mumblings, and with all our problems, and He will never love us any more than He does right now.

God's Holy Spirit fills us, empowers us, and uses us, even when we give Him blunt tools. This was David's secret! He was no superboy. The secret is found in 1 Samuel 16:13: "The Spirit of the LORD came upon David from that day forward" (KJV). David had no reason to take glory or praise for himself. Rather, he had every reason to be amazed that a person like him would be filled with the Spirit of God. That did not make David a saint in a stained-glass window. It made him a man, a man after God's own heart.

Discussion Questions

1. Do you agree that David was wrong to go beyond his father's instructions? Why or why not? Could God have dealt with Goliath some other way?

2. How have you responded to a problem without a specific "call"? What is involved in a "call" from God?

3. Do you agree that David could have dealt with Goliath by loving him? Why or why not? How does the idea of David's loving Goliath accord with God's command to Israel to destroy the inhabitants of the land (Deut. 7:2)? How does David's course of action accord with Christ's command to love your enemies (Matt. 5:44)?

4. How does the concept of presenting to God what we have rather than trying to give Him what we do not have free us from guilt, envy, jealousy, and frustration?

4

The Bittersweet Taste of Success
1 Samuel 18:1-16

Somebody once said that successful minds focus like a laser beam — to a single point. One thing is certain: success in anything depends upon a steadiness of purpose. A successful athlete, artist, musician — a successful anything — is a person who has learned to refuse to be swayed by lesser goals, however enticing they may appear to be.

David had a success mentality. Born with an unlikely start, he soon developed a determination to succeed. And he did not care what it cost, who stood in his way, or what kind of problems he had to face. He had a consuming ambition to succeed and would take on a Goliath at any time.

In chapter 3 we saw David's encounter with Goliath and learned about facets of David's personality. But now in 1 Samuel 18:1-16, the writer tells us that David reached a turning point in his life. He suddenly came into a new and surprising relationship.

Suppose you had been an invisible spectator in the Valley of Elah among the soldiers of the Israeli army. As a spectator, you would have seen this giant Philistine champion step out into the middle of the valley and shout his challenge to Israel. Suddenly, as you watched with your heart in your mouth, a shepherd boy would come out from the army of Israel, wearing no armor, carrying no weapons except a shepherd's sling and five smooth stones. Then before your astonished eyes you would see this young shepherd put one of those stones in his sling and with great dexterity twirl it around his head, let go of one end, and with amazing accuracy strike the giant's skull. And then, wonder of wonders, you would watch, amazed, as the giant crashed to the ground.

What really would you have seen? A conflict between two warriors? I do not think so. What you would have seen was success. That is what Saul saw, that is what the Israeli army saw, and that is what the people saw when they cheered and glorified him. In that one incident David was catapulted from insignificance into the limelight — from being a backwoods, downtrodden, unwanted child to a person whose back was being slapped, whose name was being passed from mouth to mouth, and whose praises were being sung.

How many nights had David lain under the stars and dreamed of success like that, just as any other neglected boy would have done? When he killed the bear or lion that attacked his sheep, there was nobody to watch — no audience. I doubt if his family even believed the story when he got back home. But this time there was an audience. Now people cheered and waved their flags, and it was intoxicating. This was a heady experience for a young man, and I doubt that David knew how to handle the new adulation. No one had ever said such things about him before. Instantly, through this incident, David the boy was gone forever. In his place was David the man, the man of blood.

As a reward for his valor, David was made court musician and a general in the army. Soon he went out and won victory after victory, and the songwriters got busy. At the top of the hit parade was this song that everybody was singing: "Saul has slain his thousands, and David his ten thousands."

Put yourself in David's position — the unloved boy, suddenly achieving popularity. What are his temptations? There is a temptation to pride, a temptation to rest on his laurels, perhaps a temptation to trade on his good name. There may have been a temptation to manipulate people, to get them to do what he had always wanted people to do for him but had never had the power to accomplish — maybe all or none of these things.

But one thing is certain: with David's success came bitterness. And this is something all of us must watch out for. If we set our sights on success, there is almost always a darker side. There is no such thing as success without alloy. Like David, we sometimes like to fantasize about success and dream about our goals and victories. But when our dearest wishes are fulfilled, we frequently find that our success turns to dust and ashes in our mouths. The success does not satisfy as we expected. It is only an illusion. One study of the problems of success showed that the drive for success produces nerve-racking tensions and conflict-ridden, frustrated lives.

In David's case, his success produced an irrational envy in the heart of King Saul. That was the bitterness in David's success. Saul was so eaten with self-love, so sick with insecurity, and so paranoid that he imagined all kinds of conspiracies being hatched against him. In a short time Saul's insecurity and irrationality got so strong that David had to flee for his life.

But out of the incident with Goliath, along with a new relationship, came a new strategy for David. Until that time, whenever David met a problem, he had only one method of dealing with it. He killed it. There was no other alternative but to kill. And that is the reaction one might expect from an "unblessed" child. David had never been given the opportunity to mature through the normal family processes. But now God stepped in and exposed David to a problem similar to the problem he had with Goliath. Then He exposed him to another, and another, and another. God did this so that David would learn a new strategy, a new way of reacting to the stresses of life. Let me illustrate God's method with a New Testament example.

Peter was a man who found himself with an unexpected crisis. (And bear in mind that the key to understanding how a person's mind works and what a person is really like is to watch what he does on the spur of the moment, in a difficult situation. What you do when you are unprepared reveals your true character.) Peter found himself alone, weak, and afraid. He was in the midst of a crowd, with all eyes turned upon him. There was a pause, then someone jabbed an accusing finger at him and said, "You were one of His disciples," and the crowd waited behind half-hidden smirks for his reaction. Peter had to make a split-second decision. What did he do? He lied. He flatly denied the accusation that he was a disciple of Christ, even when it came to him three times. Peter was put on the spot, with no opportunity to think out his response except to enact the one strategy he learned as a child and with which he had grown up.

But Jesus had called Peter to be an apostle, and no one with that kind of response to crisis would make an effective apostle. Therefore, God had to teach Peter a new strategy. And how did Jesus do that? Following His resurrection, He made a point of meeting with His disciples and stressing in advance that He wanted to meet with Peter. When they were all gathered together, Jesus looked at them and said, "You will be witnesses to Me, beginning at Jerusalem" (Acts 1:8, author's paraphrase). Jerusalem was the place where Peter had failed, and Peter would far rather have gone somewhere else and started again; but God said, "No. I'm going to present you with the same kind of problem and the same situation. You will receive the same kind of accusations, and I'm going to give you another chance to learn a new strategy — a better way of handling this problem."

Ruth Paxson's definition of forgiveness is very appropriate here: "It's being trusted again by God in the place where you have failed." Peter experienced this kind of forgiveness. He was trusted again to go to Jerusalem — the same place, the same kind of situation, and another opportunity to learn a new way of dealing with that accusation.

David also tasted this kind of forgiveness. He was trusted again by God in the area in which he had failed. In my mind, David's encounter with Goliath was a failure. Nowhere in Scripture is David praised for killing Goliath. Jesus made a number of references to David, but He never once mentioned the Goliath incident as being one of David's triumphs. I suggest that it was a spur of the moment strategy and not the best strategy. Now, what does God do? In 1 Samuel 18:28-29, we find David presented with an old problem: "When the king realized how much the Lord was with David and how immensely popular he was with all the people, he became even more afraid of him, and grew to hate him more with every passing day."

God brought across David's path another Goliath, another enemy, another challenge, another problem. This time it was the king, and what was David going to do? Kill him? After all, David was now the anointed king. He had the power and justification. But as David pondered his problem, something began to happen to him. David began to realize that there is more than one way to handle a problem. He began to realize he did not have to kill a problem to overcome it.

In 1 Samuel 19, the problem continued to increase. David was in grave danger as Saul urged his aides and his son Jonathan to assassinate David. And in verses 9 and 10 of chapter 19, we read an incredible story: "One day as Saul was sitting at home, listening to David playing the harp, suddenly the tormenting spirit from the Lord attacked him. He had his spear in his hand, and hurled it at David in an attempt to kill him." The problem was obviously getting more and more acute. Not only did Saul hate him and try to bring about his death, but now he even attempted it himself. What was David going to do? "But David dodged out of the way and fled into the night, leaving the spear imbedded in the timber of the wall." Here was a new strategy, a new method of handling a problem.

In chapter 24, we find out just how much David had grown. Unknown to Saul, David and his men were hiding in the very cave Saul chose to relieve himself in. When David realized it was Saul, he crept forward and quietly slit off the bottom of Saul's robe. But then in verse 6, David's conscience began to bother him, and he said to his men: "I shouldn't have done it." And these men who moments before were trying to persuade David to kill Saul knew something had happened to David. It was a mature David who stepped out into the sunlight and enacted his new strategy.

In verse 12, David shouted out to Saul: "The Lord will decide between us. Perhaps he will kill you for what you are trying to do to me, but I will never harm you." What was Saul's reaction to this? In verses 16-22 Saul said:

"Is it really you, my son David?" Then he began to cry. And he said to David, "You are a better man than I am, for you have repaid me good for evil. Yes, you have been wonderfully kind to me today, for when the Lord delivered me into your hand, you didn't kill me. Who else in all the world would let his enemy get away when he had him in his power? May the Lord reward you well for the kindness you have shown me today. And now I realize that you are surely going to be king, and Israel shall be yours to rule. Oh, swear to me by the Lord that when that happens you will not kill my family and destroy my line of descendants!" So David promised, and Saul went home, but David and his men went back to their cave.

Here was David's new strategy. He could have used another Goliath solution, and that would have immediately solved the problem — Saul would have been out of the way. But it would not have been the best solution for David or Israel, and certainly it would not have been the best for Saul. It was a new David that we see.

God, I believe, periodically brings problems across our pathways to teach us new strategies. Sometimes when we are faced with a problem, we do a Goliath. We march right in and kill the problem. And when we do, we get pats on the back, we get praise, and we get smiles of approval from our Christian friends. We get smiles of approval from everybody except God. And because He loves us so much, He repeats the problem in another form. He replaces our Goliath with a Saul. If you ever wonder why problems come your way, here, at least, is one reason. It is because God wants to teach us new strategies and bring us to maturity. That is grace. That is what forgiveness really is — giving us a new opportunity.

This understanding of forgiveness is one reason we all

need to watch carefully our attitudes in the face of problems. When problems come, we need wisdom to look objectively at all the events that are taking place. Instead of complaining and saying, "God, what have I done to deserve this?" ask rather, "God, what new thing about myself do You want me to learn? In what new direction do You want me to grow?"

This kind of response may be demanded of us a hundred times a day. It may happen with the people we meet, with the jobs we do, in our homes and families, or in our church involvements. Every problem, every stress, every obstacle, every frustration, every attack, every criticism is a new opportunity to grow, to learn new strategy, to mature. It may get the job done to strike out and smash the thing as David struck Goliath, but it will not teach us a thing; we will never grow.

This does not mean we will be without our temptations to lapse. David had learned this new strategy, but another situation developed that pushed him to the limits of forbearance. In 1 Samuel 25:3, there was an upstart named Nabal who cursed David. In those days, that was about the worst thing one could do to another. In verse 22, David said with fiery passion, "May God curse me if even one of his men remains alive by tomorrow morning!" In effect David said, "This is it! I can take no more! He's pushed me beyond the limits of my endurance." And if it had not been for God's special intervention in the form of Abigail, David would have unlearned the lesson he had learned in his encounter with Saul. By the grace of God, Abigail was used to open David's eyes to what he was about to do. You find David's reply to Abigail in verses 32-34:

> Bless the Lord God of Israel who has sent you to meet me today! Thank God for your good sense! Bless you for keeping me from murdering the man and carrying

out vengeance with my own hands. For I swear by the Lord, the God of Israel who has kept me from hurting you, that if you had not come out to meet me, not one of Nabal's men would be alive tomorrow morning.

There was yet another result from the Goliath incident: David accepted a new faith. Most of us want peace, and there is nothing wrong with wanting peace. But if as a result of our desire for peace we believe that all conflict is bad or that the ideal, successful Christian life must be a life free from conflict, we miss the point of the New Testament. I suggest that anybody who lives his life without conflict is not growing. I have met some Christians who seem to be sailing through life on the crest of a wave, as though the sun has always shone on them. They tell me they have perfect peace, absolute contentment, with no stress, strain, or conflict. But I am not impressed with what I see. Spiritually, they are like children. I do not mean "childlike"; I mean "childish." Conflict is absolutely essential for growth, for true success that pleases God.

Paul recognized this when he wrote to the Corinthians. He reminded them that they were, in many ways, childish. In 2 Corinthians 1:3-5 he said:

What a wonderful God we have — he is the Father of our Lord Jesus Christ, the source of every mercy, and the one who so wonderfully comforts and strengthens us in our hardships and trials. And why does he do this? So that when others are troubled, needing our sympathy and encouragement, we can pass on to them this same help and comfort God has given us. You can be sure that the more we undergo sufferings for Christ, the more he will shower us with his comfort and encouragement.

There are moments when God does intervene dramatically and suddenly in our lives. And when He does that, we have a tendency to want instant solutions to all our problems. But most often He allows trials, oppositions, and pain in our lives because He wants us to grow. Those occasions when God miraculously intervenes and suddenly removes the problem will not be growing points in our lives, because growth takes place at the point of conflict.

When God wants to make a squash, He takes six months. When He wants to make a full-grown oak, He takes a hundred years. And of David God wanted to make an oak, not a squash. He wanted David to grow, and He gave to David ten years of conflict after his victory over Goliath. There is pain when He puts us at the crossroads. Tragically, some people suffer for nothing. And sometimes those people become bitter, critical, pessimistic, and defeated. The same sun shining from the sky will melt ice and harden clay. If we handle problems as if we were clay, we will become hardened; but if we handle them as if we were ice, we will be softened. Over the years of conflict, David developed incredible patience. He kept his composure and learned patience — patience that would stand him in good stead when he became king.

David's life under Saul gave him experience that radically changed his attitude and perspective. It was, if you like, a conversion experience. God was involved in everything that was happening in David's life. David was not marching around, saying what he was doing for God; *he was being exposed to what God was doing in him.* As a result, radical changes came about in his relationship with his family. The family that had once ignored and belittled him now came to him. "So David left Gath and escaped to the cave of Adullam, where his brothers and other relatives soon joined him" (1 Sam. 22:1). I believe that when God intervenes in a person's life, there is radical change in family relationships. It is not always a healing as it was in this case. Sometimes the change will be hard, but always there will be growth.

There will be radical changes in one's interpersonal

relationships outside the family, too. David inspired strong loyalties that he could not evoke before. And that support was not the kind of popularity that had people slapping him on the back and cheering and waving and greeting him with flags. Notice 1 Samuel 22:2: "Then others began coming — those who were in any kind of trouble, such as being in debt, or merely discontented — until David was the leader of about four hundred men." He was able to inspire such confidence that his men would risk their lives to go out and get him a drink of water.

Radical changes also came about in David's relationship to God. No longer did David say, "Look, God, what I am doing in Your name! Watch me, God, as I run down this slope and meet the giant! Watch me, God, as in Your name I take a stone, and in Your name I put it in the sling, and in Your name I fell the giant!" Just because David happened to add that nice little phrase, "in Your name," did not always make it right. Jesus warned us against this attitude. "Many," He said, "will say to me in that day, 'Lord, in Your name we've cast out devils,' and 'Lord, in Your name we've done many wonderful works; in Your name we've performed miracles.' And I will say, 'Depart from me, you that work iniquity, for I never knew you'" (Matt. 7:22-23, author's paraphrase).

No, David was no longer content with *doing things in the name of God*. He was only content with what *God was doing in his life*. And in 1 Samuel 24:15 you begin to realize the impact of this, as he looked at Saul and said, "May the Lord judge as to which of us is right and punish whichever one of us is guilty. He is my lawyer and defender, and he will rescue me from your power." In chapter 26, verses 22-24, we find the same kind of reaction from David: "'Here is your spear, sir,' David replied. 'Let one of your young men come over and get it. The Lord gives his own reward for doing good and for being loyal.'" He was not interested now in praise, congratulation, and popularity. "'And I refused to kill you even when the Lord placed you in my power.'" David was telling Saul that God had exposed him, David, to Saul's unwarranted wrath to see what kind of strategy he would use. "'Now may the Lord save my life, even as I have saved yours today. May he rescue me from all my troubles.'"

David, the man, had changed. He had found a new relationship, learned a new strategy, accepted a new faith. A new man emerged, a man truly after God's own heart.

Discussion Questions

1. Since David had already been anointed by Samuel and Saul was trying to murder him, do you think David would have been justified in killing Saul when he had his many opportunities? Why or why not?

2. What problems are you struggling with now that God wants to use to help you grow? What is He trying to teach you? Do you really believe that your being in the situation is for your own good?

3. Do you agree that spiritual growth is impossible without conflict? Why or why not?

4. What does it mean to pray in Jesus' name?

5 When Life Becomes a Tangled Mess
1 Samuel 29:1-11

On one occasion a judge asked a man why he wanted to divorce his wife. "It's because my wife is too immature," he said. "You can't imagine a more childish woman. She's so immature you wouldn't believe it. I can't possibly describe her immaturity to you."

"You keep telling me how immature she is," said the judge, "but please give me an illustration of this immaturity."

The man thought for a moment and said, "Who else but an immature woman would burst into the bathroom while you're taking a bath and sink all your ships!"

Sometimes it is hard to face the truth about ourselves. It is much easier to point an accusing finger at others and let them take the blame for our problems. It is not only hard to face up to truth in everyday situations, but it is also hard to face it when we look into the Scriptures. Our twentieth century viewpoint tends to dress up Bible characters in unrealistic garb, and we fail to recognize them as real people. Yet when we peel off the veneer of veneration, we discover they were human indeed.

David is one of these. He has been a Sunday school hero for so many years that it is hard to face the truth about him.

It is so easy, for example, to say, "Oh, yes, David was a sinner"; but when we begin to analyze his sin, we do not like it.

One of the things that characterized David's early life was his immaturity, and it got him into incredible problems. David was a man with amazing ability. He had great musical talent and leadership skills. He was a poetic genius and brilliant statesman. He was a person who could inspire confidence and who possessed outstanding military prowess, but he lacked maturity.

David's early years, recorded in the book of First Samuel, are the story of a man who is stunted spiritually, mentally, and emotionally. And I believe that that immaturity contributed to his struggle for identity. David was like the butterfly struggling to get out of the cocoon. He was a man in search of himself. (The question "Who am I?" is a puzzling question for many of us. To not know one's true identity creates inner struggles and uncertainties. Frequently this causes us to be inconsistent and, strangely, it's usually the greatest problem for the person with the most potential.)

Let me extract one or two incidents from David's life to illustrate his immature search for identity. The first strategy David used when a problem occurred was to abdicate responsibility. In 1 Samuel 21:10-12, David met the Philistines, Israel's archenemies, and was face to face with a problem.

Then David hurried on, for he was fearful of Saul, and went to King Achish of Gath. But Achish's officers weren't happy about his being there. "Isn't he the top leader of Israel?" they asked. "Isn't he the one the people honor at their dances, singing, 'Saul has slain his thousands and David his ten thousands'?" David heard these comments and was afraid of what King Achish might do to him.

Here now was both a problem and an opportunity. Here

was a chance to learn a new strategy (remember from the last chapter that God let David face problems so that he could have such opportunities to grow), and what did David do?

So he pretended to be insane! He scratched on doors and let his spittle flow down his beard, until finally King Achish said to his men, "Must you bring me a madman? We already have enough of them around here! Should such a fellow as this be my guest?" [1 Sam. 21:13-15].

Throughout David's ten years of training, God continually challenged him with new problems. Curiously, David never reacted in the same way twice. When he met his first big problem, Goliath, he killed him. When he met Saul and Saul threw his javelin at him, David ran. When David had Saul under his power in the cave, he played a joke. He cut off the bottom of Saul's cloak. Later, when Saul was sleeping, David had the opportunity to steal his jug and spear, and then he could turn around to Saul and say, "Look, Saul, I'm really not such a bad fellow, am I?" And inherent in this question is another of David's problems, his sense of insecurity. David was always trying to win his way into the affection of others. We discover this in almost every one of his human encounters. It was one of the reasons he was such a bad father.

Now, in the incident with King Achish, David tried yet another strategy, one he never tried again. He played the madman. By acting out that little charade, David said, in effect, "I am not a responsible person; therefore, you can't blame me." He retreated behind bizarre behavior — a person unable to face life. He was afraid and ran, but this time within himself.

One of the most basic definitions of an adult is one who can take responsibility for his own actions. If two children playing ball happen to break a window, Johnny will say it was Billy's fault because Billy threw the ball. And Billy will say it was Johnny's fault because Johnny did not catch the ball. Each of them, from his own standpoint, is able to excuse himself and blame the other. That is childish and immature, yet that is how David retreated. The Philistines looked at David and said, "This is the man who killed ten thousand of our people." And David said, "I'm crazy, I'm not responsible. You can't blame me."

Whenever David was accused of something, he used an interesting phrase. When David took the food up to his brothers and they began to berate him, David's immediate response was, "What have I done?" (1 Sam. 17:29). Later, when David was running from Saul and he went to speak to Jonathan, David's first words were, "What have I done?" (1 Sam. 20:1). King Achish of the Philistines changed his mind about whether he would take David as one of his soldiers, and David characteristically questioned, "What have I done?" (1 Sam. 29:8). It was David's constant tendency in the early stages of his development to protest his innocence. "If anything is wrong around here, it's not my fault," he would say.

We are living today in an immature generation, a generation of people who are not prepared to take responsibility for what happens, who constantly protest their own innocence, justify themselves, make excuses, and put the blame for everything wrong on anyone but themselves. The common attitude is rather like that of Charlie Brown in "Peanuts," who said on one occasion, "My problem is that I've got parents." The tragedy with this attitude, this shrugging off of responsibility, is that it begins to build tangled and involved problems.

David's problems began with the impetuous killing of Goliath. A second problem is found in 1 Samuel 27. David kept thinking to himself, *Some day Saul is going to get me. I think I'll try my luck among the Philistines until Saul quits*

hunting for me. Then I'll finally be safe again. This was a most
peculiar reaction. David was a Hebrew, yet he joined himself to the Philistines — the Hebrews' archenemies.

It is difficult to understand why a person does what he
does. How many times have you said, "I can't understand
what made him do that?" The particular action was quite
out of character. "I've known this man for years," we say. "I
can't figure it out; it doesn't make any sense." But I suggest
that that is human nature.

When I look at my own life, I often wonder what made
me say or do something. All of us think we know ourselves, yet often our actions are inconsistent with how we
think we will react in a given situation. And when we look
at David, we find the same inconsistency. We say to him,
"Why did you go down to the Philistines, of all people?"
David, a general under King Saul, had marched time and
again against the Philistines. He had killed the Philistines'
greatest warrior. Yet when he got into a crisis, he turned his
back upon his own people and took refuge among the
Philistines. And of all the places he could have gone to, he
chose Gath, the very city from which Goliath had come. If
that was not bad enough, in 1 Samuel 28:2 we find that
David said to the king of the Philistines, "Let me come
along, too, and let me fight my own people" (author's
paraphrase). At that point David became a traitor. He did
not just leave his own people; he offered to fight against
them, alongside the Philistines. This is the David we all
admire, the real man!

What makes a man do such incredibly irrational things? I
suggest that anyone who seeks to discover himself as God
made him and intended him to be will always struggle with
periodic lapses into immaturity. One sign of immaturity is
the pendulum experience in which there is no balance in a
person's thinking. He is either all for one thing or all for the
other. Such a person bends his efforts and energies along

one particular line of action and then, for no apparent reason, drops it and goes the other way.

During the course of my ministry, I have known a number of people who have been swept into Christian fellowship. They have been fervent, excited, and involved, and they have actively testified to their faith. Then something happened and suddenly they dropped everything and went off on another tangent, doing something completely different. Often they rejected and denied their faith. Why? Jesus, of course, told us such things would happen. In Matthew 13, in His parable of the sower and the seed, Jesus told about seed that fell upon shallow ground. It was all top growth — there were no roots, no maturity. It is root growth beneath the surface that makes stability and strength.

There was no root growth in David. There was much top show — much on the surface — but the real stability, the real strength, had not yet taken hold in his life. As a result, he was always vacillating, never knowing what he was about and never knowing quite how to react. And God's purpose through those ten years of training was to give David the kind of root growth he needed before he could become king of the land.

David's struggles, struggles from which he was never entirely free, caused him to make mistakes as a father. He lavished affection on Solomon and spoiled him, with the result that Solomon himself made many mistakes as king. There was a bitter rebellion with Absalom and Amnon, who had an illicit sexual relationship with his sister, all this going on in David's own household (2 Sam. 13). Adonijah, another one of David's sons, staged a rebellion against his father. The instability and insecurity in David's household defies description. But it is here that the Word of God puts its finger upon the real crux of the problem. "His father [David, regarding Adonijah] had never checked him all his life by asking him what he meant by his conduct" (1 Kings 1:6, Moffatt). David, you see, had apparently grown up without the modeling of caring parents, and his life reflected that void.

Parents have both a great privilege and a great responsibility to give their children the seeds of strength and maturity that will make them secure people and secure in Christ. There are a number of suggestions in the book of Proverbs about how to do this. One is that there is foolishness in the heart of a child, but the rod of correction will deal with it (Prov. 22:15). Many people misquote this verse. They paraphrase it by saying, "Spare the rod and spoil the child," believing that the "rod of correction" is that which one holds in one's hand and applies to the part of the child's anatomy made for receiving the application. That is incorrect. Psalm 23 says, "Thy rod and thy staff, they *comfort* me." The shepherd never applied the rod in corporal punishment on the sheep. And the shepherd's rod is the kind of rod (it is the same Hebrew word) Proverbs 22 is talking about.

The shepherd used the rod to set clear boundaries. When the sheep moved along a dangerous mountain precipice, they were conscious of the danger and would stop, trembling with fear. But when the shepherd put down his rod and held it between the sheep and the precipice, the sheep would move on. And with amazing insight, the book of Proverbs says, "What a child needs is somebody to mark out the boundaries, to make them clear and plain." This is the kind of discipline about which the Bible speaks, the kind David never had and therefore could never give. And this is why he had so much difficulty with his family — there were no boundaries. It is only when a child knows limits that he will become secure.

Another verse frequently misapplied is Proverbs 22:6: "Train up a child in the way he should go, and when he is old he will not depart from it" (RSV). Many take this to mean that if you train up a child with exposure to the Christian church and the Christian gospel, there will come a time in his life, however much he may wander, when he will eventually return. That may or may not be true, but the emphasis should be on the word "he." "Train up a child in the way *he* should go"; or you can paraphrase it: "Train up a child in *his own* way, and when he is old, he will not depart from it." This is a recognition by the writer of the book of Proverbs that God plants within each individual a creative seed, a seed that is unique to each and every person. "Recognize the differences among your children," says Proverbs in effect. "Do not treat them all the same, because they are all different. Recognize their individual needs, and meet those needs. Recognize each child's individuality and encourage the expression of that individuality. Train up a child in *his own* way; then when he is old, he will be secure. He will be able to become mature, and he will be strong."

One of the great opportunities of life is simply the opportunity of having repeated opportunities. We may be Davids and foul up situation after situation, but God never gives up. God never left David. God never said, "David, I'm tired of you; I'm tired of the mess you're making of yourself." Rather, with profound patience, God moved in again and again and again until David gradually began to grow and mature.

We today have an opportunity to give to others the insight and strength that will enable them to grow. And we have what David did not have. We have the full measure of the grace of Jesus Christ, given to us by faith, that provides us with the resources to grow. If I may put it this way, God's grace becomes a fertilizer to our growth. It becomes the means that enables us to become strong in Christ — to go out and meet our situations as men and women in Christ.

Time and again in the New Testament, the Scriptures emphasize: "In understanding, be *men!*" Paul said, "Don't be children; don't be babies; don't just stay with milk. Grow into the meat of the Word" (author's paraphrase).

The whole purpose of Christian growth is to develop spiritual maturity. If David's life teaches us nothing else, it teaches us that God desires men — grown people — people who have nourished themselves with His Word, His Truth, who are feeding daily upon Jesus Christ in their lives — who are able to go out and meet the Goliaths of our day.

The next time you catch yourself sinking other people's ships, start to grow!

Discussion Questions

1. Why do we tend to gloss over the unpleasant truths about Bible heroes?

2. In what areas of your life do you try to abdicate the responsibility for your actions, putting the blame on someone else?

3. What motives in addition to immaturity can cause a person to act inconsistently?

4. If you had lived at the time of David and been his counselor, what advice do you think you could have given him that would have helped him to mature faster?

5. Are most people as willing to learn from their mistakes as David apparently was? Are you? Why or why not?

6 How to Handle Grief
2 Samuel 1:1-4, 17-27

I have always been loath to offer shallow, bright, and breezy solutions to profound problems. As a result, I tend to overreact in the opposite direction and become overly cautious. I am especially conscious of this as I move into this chapter on how we should handle grief. The last impression I want to create is the impression that I have the answers, that when you are in sorrow you take a simple prescription, a snappy little formula that guarantees to banish your sorrow. When I say, "How to Handle Grief," I do not mean that I am going to give you a series of steps by which you can cope with any situation. What I want to do instead is to take another look at this man David to see what happened to him when he experienced grief. I want us to see if God will reveal fresh insights from His Word and from David's experiences that will help and encourage us during our own encounters with sorrow.

We have watched David in the rough-and-tumble of life. Gradually we have been able to peel away the veneer and see that David was a man with feet of clay, very much like the rest of us. But after having destroyed some illusions about David, we now come to revealing the man's true heart. We see him in grief.

I have found that people often become truly honest with themselves during a period of sorrow. Sometimes what they learn about themselves is a shock even to them. Often they hear themselves saying things they never dreamt they even thought.

David had just returned from a battle to Ziklag. Three days later a man came from the Israeli army with the news that King Saul and his son Jonathan had both been killed in another battle. David grieved deeply.

I have read a number of biographies of David, and the thing that fascinates and puzzles me is that all the biographies completely ignore this particular facet of David's life. They never talk about his grief. There are other occasions when David grieved, and strangely they, too, are ignored by the biographers. The writers who do not ignore them merely pass over them lightly. That is a shame, because it is in his grief that we have perhaps our most reliable source of understanding of David.

In 2 Samuel 18:33, when David received the news of Absalom's death, he broke into tears and went up to his room over the gate, crying as he went, "O my son Absalom, my son, my son Absalom. If only I could have died for you! O Absalom, my son, my son." Chapter 19 goes on to tell us that when Joab and the people heard that the king was weeping and mourning for Absalom, "the joy of that day's wonderful victory was turned into deep sadness. The entire army crept back into the city as though they were ashamed and had been beaten in battle" (vv. 2-3). All the while the king covered his face with his hands, crying, "O my son Absalom! O Absalom my son, my son!" (v. 4). This reveals David's heart. David was a man of great tenderness of heart, a man of great compassion, a man of great feeling and depth.

David was a creative and complicated man, as his psalms and 2 Samuel reveal, and because of that he was rarely understood. The people did not understand his grief over Absalom. In fact, Joab, who was David's right-hand man, was infuriated by David's grief. Joab, we read, went to the king's room and said to him:

> We saved your life today and the lives of your sons, your daughters, your wives and concubines; and yet you act like this, making us feel ashamed, as though we had done something wrong. You seem to love those who hate you, and hate those who love you. Apparently we don't mean anything to you; if Absalom had lived and all of us had died, you would be happy [2 Sam. 19:5-6].

But that is not what I want to dwell on in this chapter. I want rather to pick out those aspects of David's grief that might give us insight into our own grief. It is as if we peer down the corridors of time and cry out, "David, you're a man of many deep feelings, and you've been in the darkness. Therefore, for those of us who haven't been there, can you tell us what it's like? Can you help us?"

There are two facets I want to consider. The first is disorganization; the second is reorganization. When grief first strikes us, there is always a period of disorganization. It may last a week, two weeks, or in some cases even longer.

During this period of disorganization, the first thing that happens is shock. It may last only a few hours, but it is inevitable. David experienced shock when he received the news of Saul's and Jonathan's deaths. Frequently people in shock say odd things, or their minds may suddenly go blank. Notice David's reaction when a man, fresh from the battle, told him that Saul and Jonathan were both dead. "How do you know they are dead?" said David in 2 Samuel 1:5. That was really a silly question. The man had just told David he had come from the battle. He just said he had been there. David was in shock.

When grief hits, this sense of shock acts like an anesthetic, like a coldness that descends upon your mind, a numbness. You are bewildered, in a daze, stunned. If you should ever find yourself with anyone who has received news such as David received, and the person is shocked and disoriented, be prepared for anything to happen, and be careful what you say. You may find yourself subject to some harsh treatment at his hands. Notice what happened to the man who brought the news to David (v. 15): "Then he said to one of his young men, 'Kill him!' So he ran him through with his sword and he died." Those were harsh and cruel days! Death was the man's reward for bringing such news and for claiming to have killed Saul (apparently a lie; see 1 Sam. 31:3-4). David's anger was all tied up with his grief, and in his disoriented, confused state, he could think of only one thing — kill the problem. In a way, he reverted to his old method of getting rid of problems.

Grief produces many confused emotions. Often the anger one feels during a time of bereavement is anger at oneself. Perhaps, more precisely, it is guilt. You can sense this with David when he heard about Absalom. "O, Absalom, my son, my son," he said. "If only I had died for you!" In reality David was saying, "O, if only things had been different!" There is always regret and the longing to have another chance to do things differently. Guilt is cruel and crushing; therefore it is pointless to say to somebody, "There, there — it'll all be all right some day." You cannot do that. The load is too great.

Sometimes the disorganization of grief over the impending death of a loved one so confuses that we feel anger toward the person who is dying. We shrink back, recoil in horror, and try to repress it, but it is there. Anger is sometimes expressed against anybody who happens to be near, and that is why, on occasion, there is a tendency to lash out against God. Just as a drowning man thrashes about, so a bereaved person feels himself being sucked under and overwhelmed with a situation he cannot handle. It is at this point that well-meaning friends often make a mistake.

Joab came to David in his grief and said, "Now go out there and congratulate the troops, for I swear by Jehovah that if you don't, not a single one of them will remain here during the night; then you will be worse off than you have ever been in your entire life" (2 Sam. 19:7). Joab seemed callous, but what was he doing? He was saying to David, "David, snap out of it! Come on, life's got to go on! Get involved in life again. Forget your troubles and sorrows! Go out there and meet people!"

We are not quite as callous and brutal as that. We are a little more tender. But the effect is exactly the same. We go to people in their grief and we say, "Let's talk about something else. Let's change the subject." We suggest that because we are embarrassed and find it hard to know what to say. The worst advice one can give to a person who has just received news of the loss of someone close to him is, "Don't cry. Let's talk about something happier." It would have been far better for Joab to have sat down with David and said, "David, let's talk about Absalom. Let's talk about him all you like." That is the attitude of a wise friend.

Jesus handled a grief-filled situation beautifully, offering the hope that all who die in Him have. After the crucifixion, two disciples were on their way back home from Jerusalem, on the road to Emmaus. Their Lord, in whom they had placed all their hopes and dreams, had just been crucified. They had seen Him die, and the bottom had dropped out of their lives. They were in a state of disorganization — going back home, back to where things were secure and familiar. What they did not know was that Jesus had risen from the dead; and this very One whom they had seen nailed to a cross began to walk and talk with them, but they did not recognize Him. Notice how Jesus handled their grief: "Then Jesus quoted them passage after passage from the writings of the prophets, beginning with the book of Genesis and going right through the Scriptures, explaining what the passages meant and what they said about himself" (Luke 24:27). During the entire journey, Jesus talked about the one Person for whom they were grieving.

Sometimes, in the first stage of disorganization, there is a tendency to idolize the person who is dying or has died, especially if the relationship with that person has not been good. This transformation is interestingly brought out in David's lamentation in 2 Samuel 1:23. Talking of Saul and Jonathan, David said, "How much they were loved, how wonderful they were." Is it possible that David would say this? David, who had been repeatedly threatened by Saul; David, whose life had been hounded by Saul; David, who had had a javelin thrown at him by Saul? "Ah, how much they were loved," said David. The truth is that Saul had lost the respect of the people long before, and David knew it.

C. S. Lewis, one of the great minds of this century, became a Christian fairly late in life. For the first fifty-odd years of his life, Lewis had been a bachelor. In his middle fifties he married a lady named Joy Davidman. Shortly after their marriage, Joy Lewis contracted cancer. With increasing pain, C. S. Lewis watched his wife grow weaker and weaker. Within three years of the wedding, she died. From out of this experience, C. S. Lewis wrote a book called *Grief Observed*. The opening words of that book are as follows: "Nobody ever told me."

It seems to me a tragic thing that we Christians, who are given so much insight in the Word of God about life and death, about the realities of grief, should be so reticent to speak. It is tragic to be unable to help constructively simply because we do not know or are not prepared to face those conflicting emotions about which the Bible speaks. "Nobody ever told me," said C. S. Lewis, "how much grief was like fear."

During the disorganization period there is sometimes a tendency to hide within oneself, to retreat. David put on sackcloth and ashes to think things out, but no answers came to him. When a Christian goes through grief, he is often disturbed upon discovering that he cannot find answers. Before the pain of a great loss, a Christian might say, "I don't know what it's going to be like when I face bereavement, but I believe at such a moment God's surging power will take hold of me." But then the reality of death comes and he is plunged into the grief, and there is no special power. He finds himself cold and alone, with no answers, and sometimes such a one becomes almost ashamed that he seems to be making such a poor witness.

I love the phrase, "A man can put off making up his mind, but he can't put off making up his life." Life is continuous. You do not sit and brood and try to find out all the reasons why something bad has happened before you get up and face life again. You do not do what David did in 2 Samuel 19:4: "Then the king covered his face." You do not retreat within yourself. It is only when you come out of hiding that you begin to discover that God can bring wealth out of death.

An illustration of God's bringing wealth out of death can be seen in the physical world. The Dead Sea is in the south of Israel. It is called the Dead Sea because it only receives water. There is no river going out of it, and consequently it dies. There are no fish living in it, and no vegetation surrounds it. But that is only part of the truth. There is one outlet from the Dead Sea. It is an outlet toward the sky; water is lost to evaporation. What remains is a residue of potash and other valuable chemicals. This wealth, the wealth of the Dead Sea, is only possible because the sea has died. There is no life, yet through its death, it gives wealth. When we grasp our situation in life and realize that through death God can give wealth, we begin to emerge out of the stage of disorganization into reorganization.

It is interesting that David and his friends were reorganized after the deaths of Saul and Jonathan. Notice 2 Samuel 2:1: "David then asked the Lord, 'Shall I move back to Judah?'" It was time to get reorganized. Or look at 2 Samuel 19:10, where the people were saying, "Why aren't we talking about bringing the king back?" In other words, "Let's get back into organized life."

In developing countries, the architecture of an area is determined by the materials that are readily available. The architect must make do with what is at hand; the lack of other materials produces creativity. And when someone or something precious is taken from us, we are likewise forced to survive with the resources that remain at hand. For example, David could no longer lean on Jonathan after Jonathan was killed. Jonathan had been his friend, companion, the one in whom he had confided, the one person on earth who seemed to have understood him. Then Jonathan was taken, and David had to look for other resources, to be creative. It was a period of reorganization.

As we begin to reorganize our lives after the loss of a loved one on whom we had depended, looking to God for strength, we have to remember that He often does not work things out the way we expect Him to. Mary and Martha sent for Jesus because their brother Lazarus was sick. They seem to have had some preconceived ideas about what would happen. But what happened was not what they had planned, because Jesus let Lazarus die, and they were confused. When Jesus finally went to Bethany and asked to see Mary, she went out to meet Him. John 11:31 says, "When the Jewish leaders who were at the house trying to console Mary saw her leave so hastily, they assumed she was going to Lazarus' tomb to weep." But she wasn't. She was going to a Person; she was going to Christ, believing He had the answer.

The confusing thing is that Mary's original expectations did not materialize. This is where we need to get beyond the superficial and snappy answers. We say, "Jesus has the answer," and send Mary to Jesus. Mary sends for Jesus, and Jesus lets Lazarus die. There is an expectation we receive from our faith that says, "When crisis comes, there will be help." That is true. But we make a mistake if we think we know exactly what kind of help to expect. When it does not come the way we believed it would, we are likely to say, "God has forgotten me. My prayers are not being answered; my needs are not being met." The result is disappointment.

C. S. Lewis, in *Grief Observed,* confessed that all this had happened to him. As a Christian, he knew his faith was the answer, but he could not find it. But then he finally understood and said, "Because I was so convinced what ought to happen there, I was blinded to what was really happening. I was blinded and didn't see what God was doing, because I was expecting Him to do something else" (New York: Bantam, 1976, p. 1).

There is a delightful illustration of how God may act for us contrary to our expectations in Isaiah 40:31, where the promise comes through the prophet: "They that wait upon the LORD shall renew their strength; they shall [1] mount up with wings as eagles; they shall [2] run, and not be weary; and they shall [3] walk, and not faint" (KJV). The verse shows three ways in which the strength of God can come to a person, and they will not all be present in any one situation. The strength of God may come first through ecstasy. You mount up, you seem to soar. There is overwhelming joy, the glorious joy of being caught up in the Spirit of God and lifted above circumstances and situations to where you seem to float in glory.

The second way God's strength may come is to enable you to run and not be weary. It may come not through *ecstasy* but through *energy,* through fresh strength, an unflagging enthusiasm, an ability to get on and do more than you ever thought you had the strength to do.

But Isaiah also said there is a third way in which the strength of God may come. It may enable you to walk without fainting. Now, for anyone looking for the spectacular, the idea of inching one's way along through life is rather disappointing. Who wants that sort of slow progress? It does not sound like much of a religious experience, but in times of grief and bereavement, being able to walk and not faint is what counts. David knew this. He found it to be true in his Saul-and-Jonathan bereavement experience, and he found it to be true through bereavement over Absalom. Consequently, when he came to pen the words of Psalm 23, he took note of this fact and used the same verb Isaiah used: "Yea, though I *walk* through the valley of the shadow of death."

Some people think Isaiah was confused. They say he should have told us, "Walk first, then learn how to run, and then you'll be able to fly." But that is not what Isaiah said. He said, "First of all you fly, you soar, you have the ecstasy; then you run; and then you can walk." Anybody can fly in realms of ecstasy; anybody can soar when the strength of God lifts him up above and beyond his circumstances. But the hard part comes when cruel thoughts barge in and say, "I can't stand any more. What's the use of it? I'm giving up." When you do not give up, however

— that is when you know the strength of God. That is when you realize, "Lord, I don't have wings to fly with; Lord, I don't have legs to run with. But thank You, Lord, I'm still on my feet! I have not fainted — I'm still walking through life."

Before I conclude this chapter, I want to say a word about funerals. During the course of my ministry both in England and in Canada, I have conducted some two thousand funerals. I have, therefore, participated in the grief of literally thousands of people. I am deeply concerned about many modern funeral practices. I am concerned because they make a travesty of our faith. The modern funeral hides death. The body is made to look as though it is just sleeping. This is done because we think it eases the pain of those suffering the loss. But it is also done because we cannot face death. There is also the notion that a funeral should be a quiet, somber experience. One should dress in dark clothes and creep about stealthily while syrupy music oozes throughout the building in subdued lighting, and no one speaks above a whisper.

But death is victory! Death for the Christian is graduation! A Christian funeral should not be a memorial — it should be a dedication. A memorial looks back, but a dedication looks forward, and we dedicate ourselves to the unfinished task of that member of the family we have lost. We take up and do what he would have done had he lived. But let there be joy in the funeral itself. Let there be gladness, let there be music, let there be praise, let there be worship. I say this because I believe that mourners are helped far more by a service of victory and worship through Christ than by somber faces and dismal discourses.

I know there are those who will disagree with what I

have written, and they have a perfect right to do so. They also have the privilege of planning their own funerals in whatever way they would like.

But as for me, when my graduation comes, I do not want my family to take my body into a strange and unfamiliar place. Carry my body into the church, for it was there that I was carried when I was a little child, in the arms of my mother. There in my youth I accepted Jesus Christ as my Savior; there in my adolescence I passed through the waters of baptism as a demonstration of my commitment to Christ. There in the church, in life's finest hour, I stood beside the lady who was to be my wife and took my marriage vows. There in the church, in manhood, I have been strengthened by the bread and cup symbols of the broken body and shed blood of the Lord Jesus Christ. There — please — there in the church, comfort my loved ones with a worship service worthy of the New Testament and of our resurrection faith.

Then sing! Sing as though your lungs would burst, for I will be singing with throngs of God's children. Sing! Lift up your voices and sing, "All hail the power of Jesus' name; let angels prostrate fall." Then do not talk of Norman Archer. Talk of his Savior by whom this victory is possible. Talk of his Lord, talk of His power to save and to keep. Then, when you withdraw from the church, let the organ swell in triumph with Handel's "Hallelujah Chorus." Lift up your hearts, because then I will be looking into the face of Him who loved me and gave Himself for me — King of kings and Lord of lords! And He shall reign forever — Hallelujah!

Discussion Questions

1. Do you agree that Joab was wrong in the approach that he took to David and his grief? Why or why not?

2. What differences might there be when you try to comfort someone who has lost a loved one if the mourner and his loved one are believers in Jesus Christ as opposed to unbelievers?

3. Why are Christians so reluctant to discuss death? Why would it be better to be more open about it? How do we break down the inhibitions about discussing it?

4. In what ways might God make good come out of the death of a loved one?

5. Do you agree that many modern funeral practices make a travesty of the Christian faith? Why or why not?

7 How to Handle Success
2 Samuel 5:1-12

There are today many books on the market that tell how to handle defeat, depression, loneliness, guilt, anxiety, and frustration, but almost none that tell how to cope with success. The conclusion would seem to be that successful people do not need help, but I do not believe that for a moment. I am more and more convinced that just the opposite is true. As I speak with people and discuss the deeper things of life, I find that the big problem is how to handle success. I have personally found that when things are going well, I have more problems with myself and my relationships with other people and God than I have when I am in the middle of defeat. I know I have grown more, felt closer to God, and experienced greater peace of mind when things have been black and stormy. And I have found that learning to handle defeat does not help me handle success.

How can we handle success? I would like to use David's life as an illustration of this problem. A modern journalist telling David's story might headline his copy, "Poor Farm Boy Makes Good"; or, "From Shepherd to King in Six Easy Steps." But it was not as simple as that. What the journalist fails to tell us about in such copy is David's great conflict not only with Goliath, Saul, and the Philistines, but also with himself.

In the preceding chapters we have seen how David gradually emerged from the boy to become a man, a successful man, and I want now to touch on his secret — how he handled his success.

There are three ingredients for success. First, *you must know your areas of incompetence, or weaknesses.* As I think back over my experiences as a husband and father, I am shamed by the number of occasions on which I have proved to be incompetent. I think of the times when, having charged me with the care of the household, my wife has returned to find the sink full of dishes, the potatoes burning on the stove, the stereo blaring, the phone ringing, the dog barking, the children screaming, me yelling, and heaven help the cat!

And then I look at David and see his struggle to get to the top. "Saul has slain his thousands, and David his ten thousands!" cried the crowds. He was almost there, but suddenly he slipped. Saul began to chase him, and David had to hide in caves. But then Saul was killed, and suddenly the top rung was vacant. With one bound David was there — well, almost there. There were a few mopping-up operations to be done before David was ultimately king supreme — little details like somebody else's being made king at the same time in a different place. In 2 Samuel 2:4, we read how David reached those final rungs. "And the men of Judah came, and there they anointed David king over the house of Judah" (RSV). This is the second rung from the top. But look what was happening at the same time. Verses 8-10:

> But Abner, Saul's commander-in-chief, had gone to Mahanaim to crown Saul's son Ish-bosheth as king. His territory included Gilead, Ashuri, Jezreel, Ephraim, the tribe of Benjamin, and all the rest of Israel. Ish-bosheth

was forty years old at the time. He reigned in Mahanaim for two years.

All this time the house of Judah followed David, and David was king in Hebron over the house of Judah for seven years and six months. Then in 2 Samuel 5, we discover how David ultimately reached the pinnacle. Notice verse three. The elders came to the king at Hebron, King David made a covenant with them before the Lord, and they anointed David king over Israel. He was already king over Judah; now he was king over all Israel. David was thirty years old when he began to reign, and he reigned forty years. At Hebron he reigned over Judah seven years and six months, and in Jerusalem he reigned over all Israel and Judah thirty-three years. He was at the top.

But from this point on, we become aware that David had much incompetence. As a God-fearing man, a king with enormous responsibility, he got mad at God. It happened when David decided it would be a good idea to bring the Ark to Jerusalem. The Ark was a treasured chest containing the valuable artifacts of the Jewish faith. To bring it to Jerusalem would be a great accomplishment, and he laid his plans accordingly. Nothing could go wrong. David was a great organizer and left no stone unturned — everything was worked out to the last detail. But, as always, the unexpected happened.

Along the way there was an accident, which meant everything had to stop. Read what happened in 2 Samuel 6:8. David was angry at what the Lord had done, and he said to God, "God, why are You ruining my plans? I want that Ark, and You're making it tough for me" (author's paraphrase). It was at that point that David demonstrated incompetence as the leader of God's people.

As a husband, David demonstrated his incompetence when the Ark finally arrived in Jerusalem. David was at the peak of exhilaration, and he danced and skipped and sang.

But notice the reaction of his wife in 2 Samuel 6:16: "Michal, Saul's daughter, watched from a window and saw King David leaping and dancing before the Lord; and she was filled with contempt for him." And this bad relationship with his wives went on and on, one after the other. David also had problems with his wives' ex-husbands, and in each case, he proved himself to be an incompetent husband.

With all the plots and intrigues that went on behind David's back, it seems to me incredible that David was powerless — or at least he assumed no responsibility — to deal with them. Joab, David's own general, went out and did whatever he liked. He murdered King Ish-bosheth as well as David's own son. He instituted destruction of towns and villages, and whenever David learned about such things, he did nothing more than weep and grieve and say, "Oh, naughty Joab!"

Yet in spite of all this, David has gone down in the annals of history as a success, a great man. Why? I believe one of the fundamental reasons for David's greatness is that he knew his weakness. He was well aware of his incompetence in many areas. He was no fool. Saul's problem was just the opposite. When he was confronted, he would back away and try to justify himself, and that God will not tolerate. Whenever David was confronted with his failure and incompetence, he would say, "Yes, it's true," and he would know how to repent from the bottom of his heart. That was David's great strength. When the impact of the way he brought about the murder of Uriah the Hittite to marry Bathsheba hit him, he wrote in Psalm 51:4: "Against thee [God], thee only, have I sinned, and done this evil in thy sight" (KJV). Anyone who is that honest is at once open to the grace of God.

Some people suggest that the secret of success is to know your abilities, but I disagree. The secret of success is to know your disabilities. God's ideas about leadership are radical. Jesus said, "I am among you as one that serveth." And the truly great leader is one who says, "Yes, I have failed. I have proved to be incompetent many times. I admit it, I confess it, I acknowledge it. I am not blind to it, and neither is anybody else. There is no point in putting on a mask or blustering, or making excuses."

The Christian life, you see, is not difficult — it is impossible. We cannot live it in our own strength. The glorious thing about the Christian life is that it begins at this point. It tells us we will fail; it acknowledges our weakness and incompetence, so much so that we are never surprised or caught off guard when we fail. Nor was David. But until you and I realize this, we will never know true success, growth, or maturity. We must each come to the point of being able to confess honestly our sins in specifics rather than broad generalities. It is easy enough to say, "I've sinned." But when I put my finger on my weakness and say, "This is a sign of my incompetence in these various areas," then I open the door to the full measure of the grace of the Lord Jesus Christ. That is true success. To be a success, you must know your areas of incompetence.

Second, to be a success *you must find your level of leadership*. We need leaders, but leaders must also be submissive, especially to God. We worship one God, who is made known to us in the Persons of His Son and His Holy Spirit. The Father is the symbol of authority, and the Son is the symbol of submission. Throughout His ministry, Jesus repeatedly said: "Not my will, but Thine be done! I come not to do my own will, but the will of my Father which sent me." You cannot think of God without thinking of authority, and you cannot think of God without thinking of submission. Authority and submission are interlocked in God. And because we who believe in Christ are indwelt by God the Holy Spirit, we therefore have the Spirit both of authority and of submission.

In some circles, *leadership* is a bad word. One writer said concerning this:

"Leaderless groups" emerge as a fad. "Pure equality" threatens the nation.... The real leadership is either confused or hidden,...or else the group is breaking apart.... Leaderless groups prove psychological unrealities, social impossibilities, practical monstrosities. Every group develops its own leadership; leadership is the law of the group; without leadership you have no group. Leadership is linkage: without fatherhood you lose brotherhood [Howard Butt, *The Velvet Covered Brick*, Harper & Row, 1973, p. 28].

Jesus acknowledged the existence of and need for leadership. He talked about students and teachers, caretakers and owners, servants and masters, children and parents, subjects and rulers, sons and fathers.

Now let me give an illustration of the opposite point of view, of nonsubmissive leadership. Once upon a time there was a Greek philosopher called Aristippus who wanted a favor from one of the rulers, whose name was Dionysius, ruler of the city of Syracuse. One day Aristippus presented himself to Dionysius and made his request, but Dionysius refused him. Time and again Aristippus went back to ask, and each time Dionysius refused. Now those were the days when philosophers were considered to be even more honorable than the king. The king had all the authority and power, but the philosopher had his mind. Frustrated with these rebuffs, however, Aristippus went back to Dionysius, humbled himself, and prostrated himself at Dionysius's feet. Embarrassed and overwhelmed, Dionysius stopped and listened, then gave Aristippus what he wanted. And Aristippus went away satisfied. But his fellow philosophers criticized Aristippus. "Look," they said, "you are demeaning the whole concept of our philosophy. You're dragging it in the dirt by humbling yourself before such a tyrant."

Then Aristippus made an interesting reply. "It is not my fault," he said. "The fault is with Dionysius. He hath ears in his feet."

Peter Drucker, a well-known and greatly respected management consultant, said in one of his books, "The man who stresses his downward authority is a subordinate, no matter how exalted his rank." In other words, the man who plays the Dionysius with ears in his feet — who gets his subordinates to grovel before him — is himself a subordinate, whether he realizes it or not.

This has been the concept of Scripture ever since the Word of God was first inspired — authority and submission in beautiful harmony. It was there in the very life of Christ, who stooped to wash His disciples' feet. David, a man after God's own heart, learned submission. Time and again you see it emerge. Notice an example of it in 2 Samuel 2:1: "David inquired of the Lord, 'Shall I go up into any of the cities of Judah?' And the Lord said to him, 'Go up'" (author's paraphrase). Notice how David's attitude had changed. At one time he would not have bothered to inquire anything of the Lord. He saw Goliath, put stones in his sling, and killed him. But then a new David emerged. In 2 Samuel 5:23-25 it says, "And when David inquired of the LORD, he said, 'You shall not go up; go around to their rear, and come upon them opposite the balsam trees. And when you hear the sound of marching in the tops of the balsam trees, then bestir yourself; for then the LORD has gone out before you to smite the army of the Philistines.' And David did as the LORD commanded him" (RSV). David was submissive.

A little later, in 2 Samuel 6:20-22 (this is the aftermath of Michal's sneering), we are told:

David returned to bless his household. But Michal the daughter of Saul came out to meet David, and said, "How the king of Israel honored himself today, uncovering himself today before the eyes of his servants' maids, as one of the vulgar fellows shamelessly uncovers himself!" And David said to Michal, "It was before the LORD, who chose me above your father, and above all his house, to appoint me as prince over Israel, the people of the LORD — and I will make merry before the LORD. I will make myself yet more contemptible than this, and I will be abased in your eyes; but by the maids of whom you have spoken, by them I shall be held in honor" [RSV].

Here was a man who had discovered what submission is all about. He was not concerned with the attitude of his peers. Rather, he was concerned that the handmaidens beneath him should respect him. David wanted them to know that what he did he did before God. This is an example of great leadership.

On one occasion one of my sons, his eyes flashing fire, said, "Dad, what makes you think you're right all the time? Do you think you're God or something?" To which I replied, "In *this* family I am." I have no illusions of grandeur, but I said that about myself because I am a man, and I am no more than a man. But I am no less than a man, either. Someone once said, "Parents who are willing to suffer the pain of their child's intense anger convince him that they care enough about him to compel him to act in a better way." Our parental duty, our responsibility, our authority to lead is given to us by God. Success in parenthood is leadership, sound leadership, David's kind of leadership; the kind of leadership that warrants the respect of those God has placed under our authority. Notice that we earn it. We do not claim it as a right. But authority is inseparably linked to submission.

When Jesus stood before Pilate, He said, "Pilate, you have authority over me only because it was given to you by God." This is also true for each of us, whether we are supervisors, foremen, teachers, parents, or adults of any shape and size. The authority is only ours because it has been entrusted to us by God. If we are to exercise sound authority, we have an obligation before God to be submissive to Him. But what did Pilate do? He washed his hands. He abdicated his reponsibility. And there are too many people in our society who are willing to abdicate their responsibility. This, I am sorry to say, is the case with too many parents. We must either lead where God has placed us to lead or end up with soiled hands in the water basin.

When David was prepared to take responsibility and assume leadership, he expressed his feelings in a psalm he wrote toward the end of his life. It is recorded in 2 Samuel 22:29: "Yea, thou art my lamp, O LORD, and my God lightens my darkness. Yea, by thee I can crush a troop, and by my God I can leap over a wall" (RSV). David was saying, "This is my secret. It's by my God that I do the amazing! By my God I assume authority!" And then with remarkable insight he added this other thought in verse 36: "Thou hast also given me the shield of thy salvation: and thy gentleness hath made me great" (KJV).

Third, true success demands that *you must find your level of submission*. Saul and David were kings. Each wore a crown and exercised the duties of his kingship, but there was a basic difference between them. Saul's commission was clear; his responsibilities were clear-cut; but he failed. He failed because when he was backed into a corner, he said, "I feared the people and obeyed their voice." With those words Saul revealed his incompetence, and he also showed whose opinion meant the most to him. Saul had forgotten that it was God who gave him the authority over people, and he ran scared. He chose the wrong route. Any man who yields to public pressure or the pressure of those beneath his control or care is in great danger.

This, I suggest, is the reason Saul lost his throne. He was frightened of his followers. In 1 Samuel 15:17, the prophet Samuel had Saul in a corner, a corner Saul tried to wriggle out of. "Though you are little in your own eyes," said Samuel, "are you not the head of the tribes of Israel?" (RSV). Saul had a poor self-image, and that is why his followers scared him.

When Samuel caught up with Saul, do you know what Saul was doing? "Samuel rose early to meet Saul in the morning; and it was told Samuel, 'Saul came to Carmel, and behold, he set up a monument for himself'" (RSV). Doesn't that tell you a great deal? Saul was so afraid that he built a monument to himself. To cover up his weakness, he exalted himself. And then Saul said to Samuel, "Well, I'll sacrifice to God" (author's paraphrase). "No," said Samuel, "to obey is better than sacrifice" (v. 22). "You are submitted, Saul, but to the wrong people," Samuel might well have said. Look at David by contrast. There was a time when the whole thought of submission was foreign to David. But David, because he had passed through humbling experiences, realized that to fight is often a sign of weakness and insecurity; that discretion is a better part of valor.

Our Lord was never stronger than when He stood in Pilate's hall — silent in the face of all the accusations made against Him. And David learned this important lesson: Never take advantage of another person's weakness. Mephibosheth, the grandson of Saul, lame in both feet, was brought to David, and David took him into his house. "Ah, yes," you say, "but what about poor Uriah the Hittite who had this little wife called Bathsheba that he loved so much? Didn't David take advantage of him? Wasn't that taking advantage of another person's weakness?" It was. "It appears then," you say, "that David violated his own principles." The answer is yes again. David was not a perfect man. There were times when he violated his own principles. But the difference between David and Saul was that David never put the responsibility for his failure on somebody else's shoulders. "It's true, and it is to my shame that it's true," said David. "I have failed."

What did Peter say in his epistle? "Humble yourselves therefore under the mighty hand of God, that in due time he may exalt you" (1 Pet. 5:6, RSV). In effect Peter was saying, "I know submission hurts, but it's the key to success." It cost David years of waiting. David could have sliced off Saul's head and assumed the kingdom. He could have done a "Goliath" right there. But what kind of king would he have been? He would have been a king who knew no self-control, a king who could not submit, and a king, therefore, unfit to rule.

Submission does not whittle you down, it builds you up. Submissive authority is the kind that lasts. The choice of a king for Israel was God's, and He did not choose David because David had special virtues. God chose David because David was prepared to do what God wanted him to do. It was not that David was such a great person; the flaws in his character are obvious to anybody. But David knew how to submit to God's authority in his life and therefore to become a man after God's own heart.

Discussion Questions

1. Why is it so difficult for us to handle success successfully?
2. What are your areas of incompetence? What can you learn from the life of David to help you deal with them?
3. What is involved in submissive leadership? How does it affect relationships with God and others?
4. Saul disobeyed God because the people were disobedient, and he was afraid of them. Does a leader — even a Christian leader — have to expect that those under his authority will resist his direction? Why or why not?
5. Whose authority have you been resisting, even though you know you should be submissive?

8 How to Handle Disappointment
2 Samuel 6:1-8; 7:1-11

O nce upon a time, there lived a beautiful emperor moth. To be more specific, the moth was not really living. He was all tucked up in his cocoon, waiting to be born.

The cocoon of the emperor moth is most interesting — somewhat flasklike, with a narrow, constricting neck and wider base. For the moth to be born, it must struggle, push, and eventually force its way through that narrow neck. The pressure produced by the pushing forces the moth's body fluids into its wings, making them develop fully. The result is a beautiful emperor moth.

This particular emperor moth, as it was struggling through the narrow neck of the cocoon, was being watched by a little boy. And as the moth struggled, it seemed to the child that the poor moth would never get beyond a certain point. This went on for some hours, and the little boy became increasingly concerned. "Perhaps there is something wrong," he said. "Perhaps the cocoon is too dry and it won't allow the moth to get through." Therefore, with all the pity and compassion in the world, the child took a pair of scissors and gently snipped one or two threads around the opening, just to make it a little easier for the moth to emerge. Almost immediately the moth crawled out. But as it did so, it dragged behind it a distended, ugly body and tiny, shriveled, useless wings. It was all there in perfect detail, but it was warped and immature.

We do a foolish thing when we try to handle other people's struggles or avoid our own. We sympathize with those who are struggling, and our hearts ache; but when we take our psychological scissors and snip away at some of those threads that seem to be holding them back, weaker, immature people emerge to face the world.

We seem to have a mind set today that tells us that the worst possible calamity to befall a person is struggle. Physically, we invent all kinds of labor-saving devices. Mentally, we devise teaching methods by which a child does not have to struggle to learn, so that it becomes play. We snip away at the cocoon. We do the same thing psychologically. We try to ease circumstances, to make things simpler and more comfortable for people, to enable them to emerge from their cocoons easily. The result is that we have produced a generation of people who are intellectually, emotionally, psychologically, and spiritually immature. God has given us struggle, not to be avoided, but to be part of the shaping and molding process of our lives.

David had many struggles in his life, but I want to focus in this chapter on two particular desires with which he struggled. I have chosen these two in the belief that they give us a key to what was taking place in the shaping of David's life. One desire was to move the Ark into Jerusalem, the capital city. The second was to build a temple that would be the center of Hebrew worship.

We should note first, even before looking at David's two desires in detail, that God dealt with the desires in two completely different ways. So one of the things we learn about God is His *consistent unpredictability.* Just when we think we are beginning to understand how He operates, God turns around and does something that we had not prepared for and that does not fit into our plans. We cannot predict what He will do because He knows all things, and He knows far better than we do what is in our best interest. And we also often confuse our desires with His will.

For example, there may be an occasion when you find yourself up against a brick wall, a seemingly insoluble problem, with no way out. You say, "I believe in a God of miracles; I'll see if it works." You get down on your knees and say, "God, I've got a problem, a problem from which I cannot seem to extricate myself. Only a miracle will save me." You get off your knees and what happens? Suddenly, a door appears in the wall, and you open it, go through, and you are out of your problem. Or even more miraculously, like the walls of Jericho, your brick wall falls flat and you are delivered. It is glorious, it is wonderful, and you emerge from the situation praising God for the way He has delivered you.

Then you talk to your friends and say, "Look what God has done in my life. Look how He has answered my prayer. I've put Him to the test and proved Him. It worked; it's glorious!" You are living on a tremendous spiritual high.

A few weeks later you find yourself at another impasse — another problem similar to the first. Now, of course, you can pray in faith. You have already proved what God can do, and you get down on your knees and pray. "God, You delivered me before, now let me see You work another miracle." You get up from your knees, but there is no door in the wall. There is no light over your head; the wall does not fall, and you keep pounding on it but nothing happens. And as you struggle, you begin to withdraw. The once-bright testimony fades. How can it be otherwise? How can you tell people about a God who hears and answers prayer when suddenly you find yourself pounding on walls that will not fall? How can you tell people about how God delivers when He has left you to struggle on your own? Does God know what He is doing? Doesn't He understand that you want to tell people about Him and explain how He sets people wonderfully free? God is being consistently unpredictable.

Or maybe there have been occasions in your life when you have prayed for God's blessing on your business and vowed before Him that you would be honest and fair in all your dealings with people. And God did bless you. Your business prospered, and you thanked Him for it. In situation after situation you went from strength to strength, rejoicing in God's blessing and provision.

Then suddenly you suffered a business reverse — something quite unforeseen; something for which you were not to blame caused the bottom to fall out of your business. You said: "What happened, God? Why did You bless me then and not now? I am just as faithful to You now as I was then. I wanted my business to be a testimony to all the world about how You would honor a person who was conscientious in his dealings and who was willing to give all the glory to You. Now You've left me to struggle."

Perhaps you had a Sunday school class that started off great. You had good relationships with the class members, things went well, and you had the opportunity to lead some of the children to the Lord. But halfway through the year, one or two prize students dropped out. Then discipline problems erupted and you said, "God, what are You doing with me? I pray just as earnestly now as I did at the beginning of the year. You blessed me then, why aren't You blessing me now? Why are You being so consistently unpredictable?"

I have preached sermons that have blessed and encouraged, and I praised God for it. The following Sunday I prayed, "Lord, bless again the ministry of the Word as You did last week." But what happened? You guessed it. The whole sermon fell flat on its face. I wanted to crawl away in a corner and hide. "Lord, what are You doing?" I prayed. "Why last week and not this week? I am the same person this week as I was before. I prayed as much now as I did then. What's going on around here?"

On one occasion Jesus called the Pharisees white-washed tombstones. But then He went and had dinner with one of them. That was not what the world would have expected. He called them hypocrites, and then He died for them. Many people came to Jesus for healing. It did not matter who they were or what was wrong with them; He healed them all if they had faith in Him. But when the apostle Paul, whom He obviously loved, came to Him and said, "Lord heal me," He said, "No. I'm going to show you how great My strength can be in the middle of your weakness." And Paul struggled throughout his ministry.

Now let's look at what was happening in David's life as he considered his two big ambitions. David's burning passion was to bring the Ark of God to Jerusalem. His other passion was to build a temple in which the Ark could rest and to which people could come to sacrifice and pray. Those were both worthy ambitions, yet God interfered in both of them. They were entirely different struggles, and it was hard for David to understand what God was doing with him.

In the first case, God thwarted David in anger. The Ark was on its way to Jerusalem on a cart when suddenly the Ark began to wobble. One of the attendants put out his hand to stop it from falling. It would have been a terrible thing for the Ark to have ended up in the mud. But the attendant was struck down by God, and he died on the spot. God was angry. So was David. The whole thing was a fiasco.

David's second ambition was to build the Temple, but again God intervened. His intervention was not in anger this time, but in love. God began to encourage and praise David and to remind him of all the blessings He had given him. "Although you won't get to build a temple, your son will," said God. Why this different treatment? How does one know what to expect from God? His actions seem different every day. What is God saying to us?

God is saying to us, "Listen. Please don't attempt to put Me in a strait jacket. Don't submit Me to the slide rule and the computer as if you can figure Me out — it won't work. I don't fit into any formula. Don't try and imprison Me in the neatness of your tidy mind and pigeonhole Me in your theology. One consistent thing is your inability to predict My actions. One consistent thing about Me is My creativity!" God is always creating. He did not stop creating on the sixth day. He merely rested on the seventh, and He has been creating ever since — creating new circumstances to prove His power, creating new opportunities to show His grace.

Therefore, beware of ever saying, "God did this in my life once, therefore He will do it again." He may; then again, He may not. Beware also of ever saying, "God did this in my life, therefore He will do it in yours." He may; then again, He may not. Many people stop praying because they fail to grasp this. They say, "I've prayed about it and nothing's happened. It works for other people, but it doesn't work for me." Or maybe they look back to the "good old days." "Once God did something in my life. Those were glorious, wonderful days. God was real. He blessed me, and that pleased me." And they cry out with Job, "O that I were in times past!" They long to be at the time when God was blessing them. They think it was because they were a certain kind of person that God blessed them, but now there must be something wrong with them because God is not blessing them. They fail to see that God is working just as much in their lives now as He was then — perhaps even more.

For a moment, put yourself in David's shoes. Everything he did succeeded. He went to a giant with a sling and some pebbles and killed him with one stone. He became a general in Saul's army, did battle with the enemy, and came home victorious every time. Why didn't it continue? Was there something wrong with David's faith? Not really. That is not the issue. Hebrews 11 has a long list of people, all of whom showed great faith. An important comment is made by the author in verses 39-40: "And these men of faith, though they trusted God and won his approval, none of them received all that God had promised them; for God wanted them to wait and share the even better rewards that were prepared for us." There was nothing wrong with the faith of those men and women, nothing wrong with their commitment. God honored them and approved of them, but they did not see complete victory until God called them to Himself.

What if David had known nothing but success? What if the sun had always shone upon his life? Yes, there are some places where the sun always shines, and we call them deserts. Disappointments are His appointments — God's consistent unpredictability.

As we look at these illustrations closely, we find a second premise beginning to emerge, God's *absent presence*. The Ark had great significance to the Hebrew people because it was a symbol of the presence of God. In it were the tablets of stone Moses brought down from the mountain with the Ten Commandments etched upon them, together with several other mementos of that great expedition into the promised land. And God had said that by means of and through this Ark He would communicate with His people: "And I will meet with you there and talk with you from above the place of mercy between the cherubim; and the Ark will contain the laws of my covenant. There I will tell you my commandments for the people of Israel" (Exod. 25:22). Here was God's promise that this would be the sign of His presence with them. David knew he needed to know and experience the presence of God.

But for seventy years the Ark of the Covenant had been missing. It had been captured by the Philistine army in battle. The Ark was taken into the battle because the Israelites thought they would use it as a sort of magic charm. But the plan did not work, and the enemy captured the Ark. However, the Ark created a problem for the Philistines, and they decided to give it back. To get it back to the Israelites, the Philistines used their ingenuity and made a new cart for it. Then they trundled it along to the house of Abinadab, who lived on the border between Philistia and Israel. There it stayed for seventy years. It was at this point that David decided to bring it to Jerusalem. The symbol of the presence of God was at last on its way!

But this is when the problem occurred. The new cart that David made for the Ark was not quite adequate to stand the rough journey, and the Ark began to topple. Uzzah, the attendant, put out his hand to stop it from falling and was struck down. Notice David's classic response to this incident in 2 Samuel 6:8-9: "David was angry at what the Lord had done, and named the spot 'The Place of Wrath upon Uzzah' (which it is still called to this day). David was now afraid of the Lord and asked, 'How can I ever bring the Ark home?'" He was disappointed, frustrated — naturally. "Why did this have to happen?" said David. "What better desire could I have than to bring to Jerusalem the symbol of the presence of God? I just wanted to bring that symbol to where I was. Surely God could let me do that!"

If David had been able to bring the Ark home, it would have indicated to the people that it was all right to ignore God. God had indicated just how the Ark was to be moved. It was not to be moved on a cart; rather, it was to be carried on special handles, or staves, and by special people, the Kohathite branch of the Levites, who were consecrated for that purpose. If God had not interrupted David's plans, David would have proved that you could ignore God and His laws. Without the dramatic object lesson of Uzzah's death, anyone could build a cart and bring the symbol of the presence of the Lord to himself any way he liked. (The direct cause of Uzzah's death was his violation of God's commandment that no one was to touch the Ark [Num. 4:15]. But Uzzah would not have tried to touch it if David had moved it properly.) "No," says God, "if you want My presence, it comes My way, the way I have prescribed." But sometimes we want to use our own ingenuity to engineer our way into God's presence and manipulate Him to move things our way.

There is yet another lesson to learn from this. David learned the enrichment of disappointment.

At Christmas time, we have a family custom of playing all kinds of games. This is about the only time our games emerge from the cupboard. Sometimes we get carried away with these games, and the pitch of excitement runs high. One year, one of our youngsters, after being thoroughly and fairly beaten, was on the verge of tears. In utter frustration he thumped the table and said, "But it's stupid to lose, it's stupid to lose!" Losing makes us feel small, and that is why we try to win. We hate being small. It is hard to face disappointments.

David had lost. Think how important it could have made him feel. He could have looked down on all the surrounding kings in other nations and said, "I have the symbol of the presence of God in my capital city. What have you got in yours?" Oh, how little we know ourselves, and how ugly it is when our faith makes us superior. And it may have been a "superior" faith that led David astray here.

But David's real mistake was copying the Philistines. The Philistines had made a cart, and it seemed such a good idea that David decided to do the same, contrary to God's instructions about how the Ark was to be moved. So many of our disappointments occur when we cease to be true to ourselves and fail to do what we know to be right for us. When we have poor self-images, we are especially likely to imitate others rather than do what we know to be right. We say, in effect, "God did a poor job when He created me."

As I look back over some of the major disappointments of my life, I realize that many have occurred when I have tried to engineer God's presence into my ministry by aping His most successful servants. I have tried to imitate Billy Graham's fervor, Peter Marshall's prayers, Charles Finney's power, Charles Spurgeon's theology, Martin Luther's courage, John Bunyan's imagination, and John Calvin's intellect. That is not a list of Philistine-like pagans, but it was still wrong for me to try to imitate those men. Imitation may be flattering to those we try to copy, but it only ends up in disappointment, because the presence, or power, of God is absent. It stays on the cart, and you lose your identity along the way. You are not yourself.

But there is a way to know God's power in your life. It is not by imitation but by habitation. Christ's life within you — not your hero's life, not someone else's success being indelibly stamped upon your experience, not another person's wonder-working method — is the key, the life of Christ indelibly stamped upon your heart. You need not imitate anyone or even try to copy Christ in your own strength if His life is inhabiting you. The paradox is that it is when you let Christ settle down in your life and be at home in your heart that you find the real you, the you God created you to be. You do not lose your identity — you find it in Him.

David's greatest disappointment was not being allowed to build a temple for God. We catch something of the pathos of this in 2 Samuel 7, when David said to Nathan in verse 2: "Here I am living in this beautiful cedar palace while the Ark of God is out in a tent!" "Go ahead with what you have in mind," said Nathan, "for the Lord is with you" (v. 3). Here was a typical preacher's answer. But Nathan was wrong, as preachers often are. That night the Lord said to Nathan, "Tell my servant David not to do it" (v. 5). I wonder why?

Here was David with an objective and a motive of the purest kind. There was no indication of any self-seeking. David had a vision much as we have when we first encounter Jesus Christ at the cross. We come to Him with all our hopelessness and encounter the touch of Jesus Christ on our lives. Suddenly a burden has been lifted, our sins have been washed away, and we arise from our knees new people, new creations of the Holy Spirit. And with this newness comes a new vision of what God wants to do in our lives. "Perhaps," says someone, "God wants to send me to the mission field." But God says no. He does not give a reason, and the person is puzzled.

Perhaps the most difficult time in our Christian experience is the period between God's saying no to our cherished dreams and His making clear to us why He said no. Look back and think of the number of times when you, in great faith and from the best motives, decided that if God would let you do something you would dedicate yourself to the accomplishment of the task; and then God intervened and said no. Maybe your dream was to have a home and children, and you said that if God gave them to you, you would bring up your children in the nurture and admonition of the Lord. But God said no. You remain single. Or perhaps you have had a great vision of what you could do in the name of Christ, but somehow or other, you have had a home responsibility, like a sick mother, and there is no way to get out and fulfill your vision.

If this is how you feel, or if you know of someone who feels this way, take a look at David in 1 Chronicles 22:7-10 as he talked to his son Solomon:

I wanted to build it myself, . . . but the Lord said not to do it. "You have killed too many men in great wars," he told me. "You have reddened the ground before me with blood: so you are not to build my Temple. But I will give you a son . . . who will be a man of peace. . . . He shall build my temple, and he shall be as my own son and I will be his father."

David finally learned why he could not build a temple for God, although the knowledge did not come as we might have expected (through Nathan the prophet). When the Temple was finally dedicated after being built by Solomon, Solomon remembered the experiences of his father. In 2 Chronicles 6:7-9 Solomon said: "My father David wanted to build this Temple, but the Lord said not to. It was good to have the desire, the Lord told him, but he was not the one to build it: his son was chosen for that task."

I believe that when the history of the world is complete, David will receive the glory for building the Temple that we have come to call Solomon's. All the way through the New Testament, right through to Revelation, David is the one who is exalted. David's name, not Solomon's, is in the ascendancy. I believe God will credit us for our intentions and desires, not for our successes. And when we face a disappointment, it is because God wants us to enter into the fullest part of that better thing He promised, as mentioned in Hebrews 11. David built a greater temple than he ever dreamed of. He built the line, the family tree, out of which came Jesus Christ, the Savior of the world — not out of Solomon's side of the family, but out of another side of the family altogether, traced back to David himself (Luke 3:31). God's no's are always a prelude to better things.

David's reaction to this disappointment is another classic. Before, when he was frustrated and disappointed he turned upon God in anger. But listen to a new David emerging in 2 Samuel 7:18-22a:

> David went into the Tabernacle and sat before the Lord and prayed, "O Lord God, why have you showered your blessings on such an insignificant person as I am? And now, in addition to everything else, you speak of giving me an eternal dynasty! Such generosity is far beyond any human standard! Oh, Lord God! What can I say? For you know what I am like! You are doing all these things just because you promised to and because you want to! How great you are, Lord God!"

David struggled through that narrow neck of the cocoon, and it enabled him to emerge as the fully mature emperor moth that God had planned for him to become. David never would have developed fully if somebody had come along and snipped those strands — if God had given him all his heart had desired when he wanted it. He would have come out easily. But now he could say as he did in Psalm 51:8, "Fill me with joy and gladness; let the bones which thou hast broken rejoice" (RSV). In other words, "The struggles and sufferings and disappointments You have put me through have become the very means by which I praise You."

God knew He could trust David to shine in his disappointments. Can God trust you and me like that? If we have known only bright skies, only success, He cannot trust us very far. But if He has given us sorrow and disappointment and frustration and struggles, He is showing He can trust us. Through it all, we begin to realize that although our fondest dreams crumble and we do not build what we planned to build, we *are* building. Only eternity will reveal just how much.

Discussion Questions

1. Do you agree with the suggestion that man is trying to develop a struggle-free society? Why or why not? Do you think such a society would be good? Why or why not?

2. When have you thought you knew how God was going to act in a situation, only to have Him do something different? How did you react? What did you learn from the experience?

3. Do we Christians really believe that God always acts in love in our lives, in our best interest, or is one of our basic problems a failure to trust His goodness and perfect understanding of what we need? What can we do to strengthen our faith, and what does God have to do?

4. When have you tried to engineer God's blessing on your own terms? What was the result?

5. What pure and cherished dream has God apparently forever denied you? Have you accepted His will, even if you don't know why He denied your dream?

9 A Matter of Adultery
2 Samuel 12:1-10

The subject of adultery is uncomfortable, but it is a subject that touches the raw edge of our society. I once preached a sermon on sex, and someone said to me afterward, "Fancy preaching on a subject like that with all those young people present!" I judiciously refrained from any comment. I would rather write about David and Goliath than David and Bathsheba, but if I am to be honest with Scripture, honest with David, I must probe the one incident as much as the other. One advantage of writing a book like this is that you avoid your pet themes and handle subjects you might otherwise prefer to ignore.

In the preceding chapters, we have watched David emerge from immaturity to maturity. It was a long struggle. Like the emperor moth, David emerged from his cocoon and was now king — *the* king, not just a little backwoods tribal chieftain or village head man. He was king in every sense of the word. His empire spread like a forest fire and gobbled up territories all around him. He was king of Judah, of Israel, of the Philistines, of the Moabites, of the Hittites, of the Edomites, of the Ammonites, and of every other "ite" you could lay tongue to in that part of the world.

It was in this setting that our drama took place; a drama full of color, action, intrigue, and suspense. There were plotting and assassination to compare with *The Godfather.* My version of the familiar story was inspired by John Hercus's book on David, referred to in chapter 3, in which book Hercus paints an imaginative picture of the encounters between David, Bathsheba, and Uriah the Hittite.

The drama falls naturally into three acts. Sit back now, draw back the curtain, and watch the drama unfold. Act I commences. The winter snows have melted, and the first rays of spring sunshine have begun to warm the earth and bring a touch of life, expectation, and joy into the air. There is the magic of spring, with a carpet of flowers and the song of the birds. For a man with David's temperament, this time of the year can be devastating. Once David moves, hold onto everything, because there is an earthquake coming!

We remember Goliath. One small stone and it was all over. We remember David's guerrilla attack on the Philistines by night and the disgusting performance on those uncircumcised Philistines. It seemed that David always moved in the springtime. So we watch and wait to see what new exploits David is going to be involved in. What new conquests this year? As our story begins in 2 Samuel 11:1, "In the spring of the year, the time when kings go forth to battle" (RSV), we watch breathlessly to see the direction David is going to take. Strangely, however, David — this mighty king — is fast asleep on the roof of his house. He is lying on a soft feather bed, basking in the warm sunshine and feeling an occasional cool breeze. It is the time of year when kings go forth to battle, but David is all curled up. Instead of doing battle himself, he has sent Joab and the army, and they ravage the Ammonites and besiege Rabbah. But David remains at Jerusalem. David, the leader of the most highly trained soldiers in the world up to that point, is asleep in the springtime. What has happened? Has he lost his energy? Whatever the reason, there is great wisdom in what my father said to me more times than I can remember: "Satan always finds something for idle hands to do."

People rarely get into trouble all at once. In the marriage counseling I do, in problems that develop between parents and children, in the personal problems, and in the spiritual problems I am asked to mediate, I notice that problems develop slowly. There is always a gradual sliding into trouble. There is never a sudden bolt from the blue; you do not just suddenly have a family crisis. The seeds of destruction are sown early, and then they germinate and begin to grow, until ultimately a devastating harvest is reaped.

It happened this way with David. David decided to take a year off. After all, he was getting on in years — just about fifty at this time. When you are fifty, it is time to relax a bit. You cannot do the things you used to do. It sounds so innocent, but watch carefully. Our generation is accustomed to expressing its need to relax. "You deserve a break today," we are told a thousand times. David stirs, stretches himself, and yawns. It happens early one evening, we read in 2 Samuel 11:2, when David rises from his couch and walks upon the roof of his house. Strolling along to the parapet after a lovely afternoon doze, he glances down and sees her — a vision of loveliness — Bathsheba, the wife of Uriah the Hittite. And within him, David's desires begin to stir. David, running out of steam? Don't you believe it! From his roof, he sees a woman bathing; and the woman, we read, is very beautiful.

Now David is a devious character. He wants to know who this woman is, but I imagine he wants to be discreet. He calls for his servant. Is he going to say, "Who's that down there, because I've got my eye on her?" No, he is going to say something like this: "I've not had much opportunity to get to know the neighbors around here. Who lives in that house over there? Oh, and that house over there? Really? By the way, who's living in that house down there, where that woman is? Oh, Uriah the Hittite, and Bathsheba. Very interesting, thank you very much. It's nice to get to know who your neighbors are."

Remember, David is a man of action. He is not content merely to know who she is. He is moving now. He sends messengers to get Bathsheba and bring her to him. Bathsheba is the wife of one of David's own loyal soldiers. And where is Uriah, this loyal soldier of David? Is he asleep on the roof of his house? No. He is on the battlefield, doing his job, earning enough to keep his wife and family — dreaming of Bathsheba, loving her, and looking forward to the next leave when he can come home and be with her. And David sends messengers and takes her. She comes to him and he sleeps with her. And then she goes home. The affair is over. David turns his attention to other matters. After all, he has an empire to rule, and so he pushes the whole matter out of his mind — it is over and done with. Then a day comes when he gets a message with the barest of details.

We read next in 2 Samuel 11:5 that when Bathsheba discovers she is pregnant by David, she sends a message to inform him. Now David has to think quickly. Deviously, he dispatches a memo to Joab: "Send me Uriah the Hittite." How simple it all is. The woman is pregnant. Her husband has not been home for weeks or even months. There is no way the baby could be his. The thing to do, therefore, is to get her husband home as quickly as possible. That way nobody will know whose baby it is.

The next question is how to handle Uriah. It is not plausible to bring a man back from the thick of battle for no apparent reason. He needs a good excuse for this. Verse 7 of 2 Samuel 11 says that when Uriah arrived, David asked how Joab and the army were getting along and how the war was prospering. What a quaint question! You pick a man, bring him all the way home, and ask him, "How are things going out there on the front line?" Doesn't David have some other way of getting this information? What is the matter with his intelligence service? "Just tell me how Joab is doing. I hope he's not doing too much. He has a tendency to do too much, you know, to take too much upon his own shoulders. I hope he's not overdoing it out there."

Then comes the web to trap poor, innocent Uriah. "Thank you very much for coming, Uriah. I'm sorry to have taken you away from the battle, but I was quite anxious to know how things were going. Anyway, since you are at home now, why don't you go and spend a quiet evening with your wife. You haven't been home for a long time. You can go back to the battle tomorrow."

I do not know why Uriah did not go home. If I may be permitted to go beyond the biblical account and speculate, maybe he sensed a trap. Uriah was nobody's fool. His mind is now working fast, too. *What's David got up his sleeve? What game is he playing? It's something that involves me. What can it be?* Here is David, sitting cool as he can be, and there is Uriah, standing suspicious as can be. "Thank you very much, Uriah. I won't keep you. Maybe now you would like to go home and enjoy the rest of the time with your wife."

But it does not work. Verse 9 tells us that Uriah did not go home. Rather, he stayed that night at the gateway of the palace with the other servants of the king. Uriah was trying to figure out what was going on, why King David had sent for him and encouraged him so strongly to spend the night with Bathsheba. He knew the king's palace was near his own house. He imagined that David probably could look down from the roof to where his wife often bathed in the courtyard of the house. And Uriah knew of David's several wives and his corresponding weakness for beautiful women. In other words, I believe there was no way Uriah was going to go home, because he guessed what had taken place.

The next morning at breakfast, David discovers that Uriah has not gone home, but has spent the night at the palace. Now David knows that Uriah knows, and he is desperate. Throwing caution to the wind, David summons Uriah to his chambers. "What's the matter with you?" demands David. "Why didn't you go home to your wife last night after being away so long?" Note this classic answer (Uriah, it seems to me, could be as subtle and as devious as David): "The Ark and the armies and the general and his officers are camping out in the open fields, and should I go home to wine and dine and sleep with my wife? I swear that I will never be guilty of acting like that" (2 Sam. 11:11). That is beating David at his own game!

But David knows he cannot let Uriah go. Something has got to be done. "Well, stay here tonight, and tomorrow you may return to the army," says David. *Maybe Uriah will break down tonight and go home — that's all I need*, thinks David. But Uriah stays around the palace, never going near his home. David is beside himself. Then he gets an idea. *If I can get him to dinner*, thinks David, *I can get him drunk. Then he won't know what he is doing, and everything will be all right.* But David is no pharmacist, and the alcohol has an effect completely opposite to anything he hoped to arouse in Uriah. It puts Uriah fast asleep, and he sleeps at the entrance of the palace.

This time David knows he is beaten. In the morning he says to Uriah, "It's time to go back to battle again. And I would like you to take this important message with you to Joab. It's sealed with my seal and must be put into nobody's hand but the general's. Make sure it is delivered to him only." The letter instructs Joab to put Uriah at the front of the hottest part of the battle, then pull back and leave him there to die. Joab assigns Uriah to a spot closest to the besieged city, where he knows the enemy's best men are hiding, and Uriah is killed. In a final sordid move in this part of the story, David then sends for Bathsheba, the widow of the man he has murdered, and makes her yet another of his wives.

David, the mighty conqueror, is defeated by his own passions. When Saul was killed, David wrote a lamentation, saying, "How are the mighty fallen." He might well have written it for himself.

Act I closes. But Act II becomes equally dramatic. "Nathan the prophet is here to see you, your majesty." King David wraps his royal robes around him and seats himself upon his throne, ready to receive the honored prophet of God. Nathan is ushered into his presence.

Nathan is no fool, either, and he knows you have got to be skillful and indirect when you confront David. It is no good going up to David and saying, "God knows what you've done with Bathsheba." You could not do that with David. You have got to come from another angle, and Nathan decides to force David to admit his sin by flattering him. David still has a high opinion of himself and fancies himself a counselor, able to sort out other people's problems.

"I've a problem to handle," says Nathan. "There are two people living in my community — one is wealthy and one is poor. They live next door to each other, and there is a problem I can't handle, so I've come to you for advice."

"Very well," says David, "tell me your problem and I'll see what I can do."

"Well," says Nathan, "the wealthy person has flocks, herds — he can't even count them, there are so many. His sheep run everywhere. But the poor man has only one little lamb. It's the family pet. It has grown up with the children, and they love it. Now it so happened that the wealthy man had one of his friends visit him from out of town, and this friend stayed the night. That evening the wealthy man put on a banquet, and he decided he needed a lamb for the banquet. But instead of taking one of his own lambs, of which he had thousands, he went next door, stole the pet lamb that belonged to the poor man, killed it, and served it to his guest. How would you resolve this?"

David is furious. "That such a thing should be going on in my kingdom is unthinkable. Such a person is not worthy to live. He must restore four times over what he has taken. I won't tolerate this kind of behavior in my kingdom! Who is he?"

And Nathan responds, "Thou art the man!" Out of his own mouth David convicts himself. He had thought that perhaps Joab knew of his indiscretion, but Joab could be trusted to keep quiet. However, Nathan also knows, and so does God. With this one courageous statement by Nathan, David's world comes crashing down around his ears, and he is a truly broken man.

There must have been a long silence as David grappled with this statement. Finally he makes this statement: "I have sinned against the Lord." Six simple words were all he said, but they were six words that marked a turning point in David's life. Kings, rulers, and presidents can cover up their wrongdoings to the point of being ridiculous, but eventually things have a way of catching up. Have you ever been in a situation of knowing there is something wrong in your life and hiding it, but then someone finds out and it comes to the surface? How did you handle it?

David could have exploded and said, "Nathan, you are a liar! How dare you make such an accusation against me, the king!" David could have put on a big act, but here is where you see David's emerging maturity. He is at least honest enough to admit his guilt. When God does business with a person, He is not impressed by blustering or maneuvering or camouflage. It is only when we get to the point that we will say with David, "I have sinned," that God is able to move in. Things begin to happen. This point of confession of guilt is one of the most valuable spiritual experiences, because when a person is big enough to become small enough, he starts to grow — really grow! Nobody ever yet came to Christ as anything but a sinner.

David is now left alone with God. He is going to endure a lot of pain in the years to come. His family will desert him, despise him, and rebel against him. He will be faced with bereavement and sorrow, distress and agony. His insecurity and immaturity over the years have been exhibited in his marrying many wives, thinking he could find peace of mind and heart in numbers. But he has found that there is no safety in numbers. God made the rules, and David violated them. God knew what He was doing when He set out those rules. He made them not because He wanted to be an authoritarian, but because He knew how He had created man and what kind of rules were necessary to make man realize his full potential. God is not a spoilsport when He says, "They two shall be as one flesh." There should be one husband and one wife. He says this is the way to find harmony. This is the way to grow.

And now like a flood it all comes back to David. This is the same David who a few years earlier said, "I will walk within my house with a perfect heart. I will set no wicked thing before my eyes (Psalm 101:2-3, author's paraphrase). Each of us needs to be most careful of unguarded moments and innocent little relationships that seem so harmless yet leave us vulnerable. It is not usually big things that lead to spiritual downfall; it is not the sudden attack. Rather, little, insidious things that appear to be innocent (such as spending a lazy spring afternoon on the palace roof) start those steps downward that lead eventually to distress and despair.

And now Act III. It is a beautiful scene. Here we see an

exceptionally gifted man, a great genius who had been lifted up from a shepherd to a king. But this same person who wrecked his life with gross stupidity is now on his knees before God, finding relief. And on his knees David creates one of the most beautiful psalms of all time. Psalm 51 has been one of the most treasured spiritual possessions of saints down through the centuries. The psalm has this preface: "It was written after Nathan the prophet had come to inform David of God's judgment against him because of his adultery with Bathsheba and his murder of Uriah, her husband." David, in this statement of brokenness, cries out: "O loving and kind God, have mercy. Have pity upon me and take away the awful stain of my transgressions. Oh, wash me, cleanse me from this guilt. Let me be pure again" (vv. 1-2). All the way through this psalm, David makes no reference to Bathsheba, no reference to Uriah, and none even to the baby that died shortly after birth or to Nathan — only to God. The psalm shows a man wrestling with his God and with guilt he is not afraid to face. He is not prepared to bury it and pretend it does not exist. He is big enough to confess and acknowledge it for what it is. May God give us the strength to be such men.

As David grapples with his guilt, his mind goes over and over the same old problem. "I admit my shameful deed — it haunts me day and night" (v. 3). Oh, if someone could come and take it all away as though it had never been. "Sprinkle me with the cleansing blood," says David, "and I shall be clean again. Wash me and I shall be whiter than snow" (v. 7). Oh, how he longs for those happier days in verse 8: "Give me back my joy again."

What can I do to put things right again? I cannot bring Uriah back from the dead. I cannot return Bathsheba's husband to her. I cannot even raise the baby that I produced so wrongfully. If only I could undo the whole thing; but I cannot. I wish there was something I could do. Is there some penance I could serve? Some sacrifice I could make? "You don't want penance; if you did, how gladly I would do it! You aren't interested in offerings" (v. 16). Then comes a beautiful ray of insight: "It is a broken spirit you want. . . . A broken and contrite heart, O God, you will not ignore" (v. 17). In his heartrending confession of need, weakness, and guilt, David finds a new relationship with his God. David is called a man after God's own heart, not because he lived as God would live, not because he did the things God would do, but because he knew his God. He knew what God wanted from him. He knew God would not turn His back upon him, even though he had sunk to the very depths of despair, even though he had broken his promises and his standards.

He knew that when he came to such a God, truly humbled, God would welcome him. And what God did with David He will do for you and me. If the cross of Jesus Christ means anything at all, it means the blood has been shed so that we might be washed as though our sins never had happened, as though there had never been that "ewe lamb," as though there had been perfect innocence. And when God looks upon me through the merits of Jesus Christ, all He sees is the purity of Christ. It does not matter how light or heavy my burden of guilt may be. I can find what David found — that God will not despise a contrite heart, a person who comes to Him in need and says, "Lord, I have sinned." He will be cleansed; he will be washed through the blood of Jesus Christ. This is the glory of the gospel.

Discussion Questions

1. Do you agree that Uriah had figured out what had happened between David and Bathsheba? How do you think you would have reacted in Uriah's place, remembering that David was a sovereign, with life and death authority over his subjects?

2. Do you think Joab was right in obeying David's order to murder Uriah? What could Joab have done if he did not want to carry out the order?

3. Was David right in marrying Bathsheba after Uriah's death, in light of her being pregnant with his child? If not, what should he have done for her?

4. Do you think it was fair of God to take the innocent child's life? Why did He do that?

5. We find it easy to fault David for what he did with Bathsheba and Uriah, but how guilty are we of the same offenses, based on Matthew 5:21-22, 27-28?

10 Friends Turn Against You
2 Samuel 18:24-33

Most preschool children are highly creative. They draw funny pictures, tell imaginative stories, and sing funny songs. In every way they are delightfully uninhibited. There is a sense of wonder and awe to their world. Then comes school, and gradually they learn to conform. They develop awkwardness and inhibitions. The world begins to lose its magic, and the naturalness is replaced by artificiality.

What blocks creativity in children? Parents? Teachers? Toys? Television? In a way, all these are to blame. But underlying all of them is our cultural injunction to conform. Christians seem to be particularly guilty of demanding conformity. Many tend to regard their faith as a closed system in which all the answers are in. Accurately, we attest the Scriptures to be our sole authority in matters of faith and practice, but in so doing, we forget that the God we worship is the most creative Person in the universe.

If we come to our children with a series of dead ends, we make it impossible for them truly to know and open themselves to the God of love and creativity. Some years ago a study on creativity was conducted at the University of California at Berkeley. One interesting conclusion of the study was that the creative person is usually able to solve his problems more effectively than the uncreative person, because the creative person is prepared to examine a whole range of possible solutions.

As we look into David's life, we see a person who expressed a high degree of musical and poetic creativity. But in every other dimension, his creativity was gradually sapped from him. We have seen his lack of creativity in the way he handled his problems. In a way, he developed a stereotyped attitude toward life. God's work, therefore, was to set David free and restore in him the image of God and His creativity. As David matured, God gave him an openness that enabled him to see alternate, better ways to handle problems; and as David responded to those new possibilities in his life, he began to become a man after God's own heart.

There are many facets to the gospel of Jesus Christ. One facet restores the relationship between God and man, lifts the burden of oppressive guilt, and cleanses man from sin. Another facet is a new liberty and creativity given to the person rightly related to God in Christ. This second facet becomes increasingly evident in the life of a person who willingly submits to God and His Word of truth.

But for David, it did not quite work out that simply. Even after many experiences with God, there were still inhibited and stereotyped areas in David's life. And this showed up most clearly in the way he handled his family and friends. Ultimately, David's children were emotionally scarred and guilty of great antisocial behavior. They were children in whom creativity, the ability to find better, godly ways of conduct, had been destroyed by an uncreative father. David's children had little modeling of how to handle their problems, resulting in chaos for themselves and almost everyone around them.

When unpleasant things happen to us, we sometimes complain about being victims of circumstance. "If things were different, I would be different" is a familiar refrain from those struggling with difficulties. The problem with such an attitude is that we forget that God allows such circumstances to exist so that His power can creatively work through us. Second Corinthians 12:10 says, in part, "The less I have, the more I depend on him." Unfortunately, most of us handle our sufferings uncreatively; so uncreatively, in fact, that we treat adverse circumstances as intruders; whereas James 1:2-4 says we ought to welcome them as friends. There is no growth of character without pain and suffering, which means none of us should waste his suffering in uncreative bitterness and complaining.

Let's look at David and see how responsible he was for the breakdown between himself and his family and friends. As David examined his family, he could easily have said, "No father ever had to put up with children like mine!" And he would have been right. Or he could have said, "No man has received such lack of respect and loyalty from those he has befriended." And again he would have been right. But at the same time, David's own attitudes created his problems. I would like to examine three reasons why I believe this is true.

First, *David's anger got in his way.* An observer in David's household could easily have said, "David, do you know what's going on in your own house? Do you know that your eldest son has just raped your daughter?" All the details are there in 2 Samuel 13:1-14 — all the ugliness, deceit, and physical force. All this was taking place under David's roof, and when David learned of it he was very angry. But the interesting thing is that David did nothing. This is a typical reaction of a person who cannot handle a problem decisively; of a person whose creativity has been destroyed. He just gets terribly angry.

We should thank God for the capacity to feel anger. It is an important signal that something is wrong; there is a situation that needs attention. Scripture comes through for us interestingly and practically, too, showing us that anger must be expressed in decisive, creative action. Let me illustrate.

In the Sermon on the Mount, Jesus talked about how a believer is to respond to someone who slaps him on the cheek (Matt. 5:39). Jesus said he is to turn the other cheek. But notice how Jesus expressed this. He said that if somebody slaps you on the *right* cheek, turn the other, too. The problem is that it is impossible to strike a person on the right cheek if you are right-handed unless you do it with the back of your hand. This is most significant, because a slap with the back of the hand in the time of Christ was the supreme insult. What Jesus said, then, was that when you receive an insult of insults, your reaction is naturally going to be anger. The question is, what are you going to do with that anger? How are you going to control it?

This suggestion by Jesus that we turn the other cheek has a practical application to everyday life. When you suggest that it is bedtime to most preteens, for example, their response is frequently explosive. "Mom, you're always telling me what to do!" And this attitude goes right through the teenage years, and in many people, on into adulthood. What happens when your youngster becomes angry? Most people counterattack and become angry in return. What Jesus is saying is that when someone causes anger within you, do not have such a frail ego that you have to counterattack. Rather, take decisive action, but not destructive action. Be creative; turn the other cheek. In this way, *you* will be in control of the situation.

In Matthew 5:41, Jesus gave yet another illustration, perhaps even more vivid and profound than the first: "If anybody compels you to carry his baggage for a mile, you carry it for two" (author's paraphrase). This was a familiar scene during the Roman occupation. It was part of the Roman occupational law that any soldier could press a civilian into service to carry his baggage, but only for one mile. This law infuriated the Jews and caused them to seethe with every step of that required mile. "Now," said Jesus, "how do you handle this kind of anger? Are you going to let it eat away at you? No! Listen, when you're compelled by Roman law to carry that baggage for one mile, be creative. Carry it two! Then who's in control of the situation? You are, because *you* have taken the decisive action."

David needed this advice when he faced the situation in 2 Samuel 13 that was tearing him apart. Uncreatively, David became angry but did nothing. Sometimes parents who are distressed over the way they handle their children may say, "I do nothing but yell and scream at my kids. I just can't seem to break the pattern." Paul made an interesting comment in Ephesians 6:4 when he said, "Do not exasperate your children" (NIV). Many of our problems as parents arise because we train our children to be disobedient. We do not intend to, but that is how it ends up.

Suppose friends drop in for the evening. You sit in the living room and your children are in the family room, looking at television. As you well know, this generation is half deaf, and not only is the volume on full blast, but an argument begins. The television and your children's voices penetrate the living room and disturb your conversation. You enter the family room and ask the children to turn down the television and be quiet. "We are trying to entertain our guests," you say, "and we can't hear ourselves think." You walk out and shut the door. It is quiet for maybe twenty seconds, and then gradually the volume builds up again. This time you go in mad and say, "Listen, I've told you once. How many more times do I have to tell you to be quiet?" Back to the living room you go, and this time the quiet lasts thirty seconds. The third time you go in you are frothing at the mouth and become physical with the disobedient children. And when the free-for-all is over, the children know from experience that this is the time to be quiet! Your children have learned that the first two warnings do not count. All that happens is that you get angry. And that is the way we exasperate our children and teach them disobedience.

A more creative way to handle a situation like that would be to say (the first time), "Listen, you're in this room and we're in that room. We aren't making so much noise that you can't hear the television, and we don't want you to make so much noise that we can't hear ourselves speak. Please turn the volume down and stop arguing, or the television goes off." The second time you go in you take decisive action. "OK, you've been warned; the television goes off for the rest of the evening." The next second after such action is always predictable. The parent receives the full blast of the children's angry protests. A secure parent, however, will not be intimidated. If the children know a parent will really take decisive action for disobedience after a fair warning, they are far less likely to be exasperated or resentful. They know where they stand and what action follows their disobedience.

David, on the other hand, knew little of this kind of security. His response to disobedience and overindulgence was anger, but an anger that did nothing. And the victims of his indecision were his children, especially Absalom. Absalom was the innocent party in the foul deed. His older half-brother Amnon was the guilty one. But Absalom was close to his sister, and when David took no punitive action against Amnon, Absalom's revengeful hatred against Amnon began to smolder. David knew he should take decisive action, but his anger got in the way.

David's second problem was his guilt. It also got in his way. We become angry with other people because we see our weaknesses reflected in them. This is especially true when dealing with our children. If one of our weaknesses comes out in our children, the pain and frustration we have experienced in trying to overcome the particular weakness block our ability to effectively deal with our children, and we react in anger.

I know from personal experience that this is true. When one of my sons comes home with his report card that says, "Has the ability, but lacks concentration," I get angry; but I do nothing because I know history is repeating itself. When I look at my children, I see certain strengths, abilities, and other qualities. I also see certain defects. If I were to itemize them I would put them into two categories — my weaknesses and my wife's weaknesses. When I see my wife's defects in my children I am concerned, but I find I can deal with them creatively. But when I see my own weaknesses in my children, I just get angry. I find that my wife becomes most angry when she sees her weaknesses in our children, yet she can deal creatively with those weaknesses that come from me. Perhaps families should write down who is responsible for what! We could then share the responsibility creatively for those areas that need the most creative attention.

"David," we say, "your son made you angry, but what precipitated this? It was gross sexual immorality! David, you're angry, but you do nothing because of your own guilt. You know very well that what came out of Amnon was your own immorality — your involvement with Bathsheba. David, because you feel guilty, you do nothing."

This is not the end of our story. Absalom, the innocent brother, incensed over his sister's treatment by Amnon, repressed his anger because he was living in an atmosphere in which it would have been politically unwise to express it openly. For two years he inwardly fumed and fretted. But Absalom was also a chip off the old block, and he, too, knew how to be evasive, subtle, and scheming. So he planned a party to which he invited David, knowing full well that David could not go. "'Well, then,' said Absalom, 'if you can't come, how about sending my brother Amnon instead?'" (2 Sam. 13:26). "Why Amnon?" the king asked. But Absalom kept urging until the king finally agreed. Whereupon, "Absalom told his men [in v. 28], 'Wait until Amnon gets drunk, then, at my signal, kill him.'" Here was David again — the only way to handle a problem is to kill it. "Don't be afraid," said Absalom. "I'm the one who gives orders around here, and this is a command. Take courage and do it!" And they did.

How did this affect David? In verse 31 it says, "The king jumped up, ripped off his robe, and fell prostrate to the ground." But notice that David again did nothing. Absalom had murdered his brother, but all David did was to become angry. The reason David was paralyzed was his awareness of his own sin. He, too, had been guilty of murder when he engineered the death of Uriah the Hittite.

We sometimes make the false assumption that time makes us forget. It does not, and it certainly does not diminish our guilt. The memory of the event itself may be repressed, but the feelings of guilt remain. The problem with guilt is that it immobilizes us as it did David. Every thought, every emotion, and every event has some permanent influence on the personality. David's guilt paralyzed him, and he could do nothing. Furthermore, complications began to appear.

After Absalom had Amnon killed, he kept his distance from David. But David's general, Joab, devised a plan to get Absalom back into David's good favor. In 2 Samuel 14:1-13, Joab sent for a woman of Tekoa, who said (author's paraphrase): "Your majesty, I've got a problem [purely a fictional thing]. I have two sons — one of them has killed the other, leaving me with only one son, and he is a murderer. All my friends and relatives are hounding him to death, but if they kill him, I will have no sons. So, your majesty, I've come to ask you to save the life of my guilty son."

"I will," said David. "As long as I am king around here, no harm will befall your son, even though he be guilty. Rest assured, I will protect and take care of him" (author's paraphrase).

Then the woman said, "Your majesty, please, why don't you practice what you preach? How about your treatment of Absalom?" (author's paraphrase). And David was paralyzed.

David's guilt made it impossible for him to take decisive or creative action, and it made it impossible for him to forgive. In verse 24, after he was pressured by this subtlety into bringing Absalom back, David said, "He [Absalom] may go to his own quarters, but he must never come here. I refuse to see him." This was tantamount to the prodigal son's coming back to his father and his father saying, "I see you've come to your senses. That's good, but you're no longer my son. Go to the kitchen and you'll find some cold leftover potatoes." David could not forgive Absalom because he had never forgiven himself.

Many Christians get all twisted up at this point. They have their guilt, they come to God, they confess their sin, are forgiven, and yet the guilt still paralyzes them. Forgiveness is one of the most powerful forces ever let loose in the world. If you find yourself saying to somebody, "I can never forgive you for what you did to me," ask yourself what you are feeling guilty about. Why is it that God can forgive so readily? Why is it that Jesus Christ on the cross could utter those words without reservation, "Father, forgive them, for they know not what they do"? The reason God can forgive is because God has no guilt. Therefore, God can handle any situation and devise creative means to reconcile man.

There is an interesting sidelight to this. It is difficult to ask for forgiveness, but it is also difficult to give genuine forgiveness. Somebody may come to you sometime and say, "Jack, I'm sorry for what I did to you, for the attitude I adopted. I was wrong and mean, and I want to ask your forgiveness." You may reply, "Oh, that's OK. Just forget it

— didn't bother me at all." That is a lie, of course, and it is not forgiveness. It is the reverse. Oh, how difficult it is to forgive.

In 2 Samuel 14:33, David at last summoned Absalom, who came and bowed low before the king; and David kissed him. But I would suggest that this was not forgiveness. It was neither asked for nor given, and Absalom knew it. We need an honesty that says to a person who has asked our forgiveness, "Yes, what you did hurt me, and I did have some resentment. It bothered me, but I want our relationship to be healed. I appreciate your asking for my forgiveness, and I forgive you." This is God's kind of forgiveness. God is not so insecure that He would turn to us and say, like a benign old grandfather, sitting in His rocking chair and giving a knowing little wink to His children on earth who perform a little accident or indiscretion, "Oh, it's all right. It doesn't bother me." *It does bother God.* God tells us it hurts. But when we say to Him, "Father, forgive me," He says, "Yes, it hurt. It hurt to the death of My Son upon the cross, but I forgive — utterly, completely." And God remembers it no more.

Finally, *David's lack of creativity was the result of his failure.* It also got in David's way. Let me give you a little cameo. Here was Absalom — unforgiven, still guilty, resentful, a product of mismanagement within his home. See 2 Samuel 15:1: "Absalom then bought a magnificent chariot and chariot horses, and hired fifty footmen to run ahead of him." He was going to play the grandiose prince. He got up early every morning and went out to the gate of the city. When anyone came to bring a case to the king for trial, Absalom called him over and expressed interest. "I can see you were right in this matter," he would say. "It's unfortunate the king doesn't have anyone to assist him in hearing these cases. I surely wish I were the judge; then anyone with a lawsuit could come to me, and I would give him justice" (author's paraphrase). And so we read, "And in this way,

Absalom stole the hearts of the people of Israel" (author's paraphrase).

In verse 10, Absalom went to Hebron. While he was there, he sent spies to every part of Israel to incite rebellion against the king. "'As soon as you hear trumpets,' the message read, 'you will know that Absalom has been crowned in Hebron.'" And then the conspiracy erupted, and David's family, friends, and trusted advisers all turned on him. People he had helped and comforted spat on him and cursed him, and once again David became a fugitive.

Verse 14 of chapter 15 says, "Then we must flee at once or it will be too late!" What an odd attitude for the king to take. Why did David handle his problem this way and suddenly become a fugitive? I cannot help but feel that David was never better than when he was a fugitive. He looked back over his life and saw the mess he had gotten himself into — the mess with his wives, his children, the rest of his relatives, and his country. The nation was in a civil war, the empire was crumbling, and he longed for the "good old days" when he was running for his life from the anger of Saul. David was never stronger than when he was running from Saul, hiding out in the desert and living in caves. In the midst of this great failure, David wanted a little crowd of trusted and ardent followers around him so that he could be the man he used to be. This is a most subtle temptation.

When Christians make a mess of their lives, they often, like David, try to turn back the clock to the "good old days." But that is never an answer to failure. David wrote Psalm 3 when he fled from his son Absalom. Notice the theme in verses 1-5.

O Lord, so many are against me. So many seek to harm me. I have so many enemies. So many say that God will never help me. But Lord, you are my shield, my glory, and my only hope. You alone can lift my head, now bowed in shame. I cried out to the Lord, and he heard me from his Temple in Jerusalem. Then I lay down and slept in peace and woke up safely, for the Lord was watching over me.

David had been called, appointed, and anointed by God to rule, yet he allowed himself to be manipulated by his circumstances. Have you ever felt like David — that your family has turned against you; that your friends have forsaken you; that you have been misunderstood, misquoted, and misinterpreted; that you have received a lot of ill treatment you do not deserve? Have you ever felt paralyzed in the face of it — paralyzed by your anger, guilt, or failure; like David, so anxious to preserve what little you have left? But you say to your Joab, "In spite of everything, don't let Absalom die."

But Absalom did die, killed by the sword of Joab. And David's lament was one of the most pathetic events in the whole of his life: "Then the king broke into tears, went up to his room over the gate, crying as he went. 'O my son Absalom, my son, my son Absalom. If only I could have died for you! O Absalom, my son, my son'" (2 Sam. 18:33). I believe this was the cry of a brokenhearted man; the cry of a man full of remorse; the cry of a man who wishes he could turn back the clock and have a second chance to be a different kind of father.

Thank God for the gospel of Jesus Christ! It is a gospel for failures; it is a gospel for people who are paralyzed by their failure, guilt, and anger. Thank God that I can point you to Jesus Christ and say, "Behold the Lamb of God, who takes away the sin of the world." Thank God that I can offer you a release in Him, and in His power a new start, a new beginning. If only David could have known this, he would have at this point emerged a different man. Thank God for that gloriously creative moment in history when Jesus rose from the grave and brought into being the miracle of new birth, the new opportunity, and fresh beginning. "If any man be in Christ, he is *a new creation*. Old things are passed away, all things have become new" (2 Cor. 5:17, author's paraphrase).

We may have our anger, guilt, and failure as David did, but we do not have to pour out a lament and grovel in our misery. We can come to the one place where we know there is healing, acceptance, and peace; where Jesus smiles down at us from the cross and says, "This I have done to give you life. Rise up and live."

Discussion Questions

1. In this chapter, creativity is defined as the ability to find new and better ways of doing things. Do you agree with that definition and its application to the spiritual life? Why or why not? In what areas of your life do you need to be more creative?

2. How should David have reacted to the sins of Amnon and Absalom? Do you, like David, tend to get angry about things but do nothing? What can you learn from David's life to help you overcome that tendency?

3. Which of your parents' weaknesses do you see in yourself? Which of your weaknesses do you see in your children?

4. To whom do you need to give genuine forgiveness, having given only half-hearted forgiveness before? Whose forgiveness do you need to seek?

5. What memories of past success do you cling to, using them as an escape from present problems? What does David's experience suggest you need to do with them?

11 God Didn't Answer My Prayer
2 Samuel 12:13-23

When taking his leave from King Louis XIV of France, Marechal Villars is reported to have said, "Lord, defend me from my friends. I can defend myself from my enemies." Prayer is a little like this. Many Christian people, from the best motives in the world, make extravagant claims about what prayer can do in a person's life, raising false hopes in others. They lay hold of such promises as, "Whatsoever ye shall ask in my name, that will I do" (John 14:13*a*, KJV). They misunderstand those words of Jesus and so apply them in ways He never intended, thereby creating confusion, bewilderment, and doubt.

Mark Twain, in his inimitable style, dealt with this problem of unanswered prayer in his book *Huckleberry Finn* when he put into Huck's mouth these words:

Miss Watson, she took me in the closet and prayed, but nothing come of it. She told me to pray and whatever I asked I would get it, but it warn't so. I tried it. Once I got a fish line, but no hooks. It warn't any good to me without hooks. I tried for the hooks three or four times, but somehow I couldn't make it work. By and by one day I asked Miss Watson to try for me, but she said I was a

124

fool. She never told me why and I couldn't make it out no way. I set down one time back in the woods and had a long think about it and said to myself, "If a body can get anything they pray for, why don't Deacon Winn get back the money he lost on pork? Why can't the widow get back her silver snuff box that was stole? Why can't Miss Watson fat up? No," says I to myself, "there ain't nothing in it."

People have prayed for fine weather, and it has rained in torrents. People have prayed for health and have landed in hospitals. People have prayed to live and then died. As we go through David's life, we find a pathetic story of a father who prayed for his son to live. In 2 Samuel 12, we read that the Lord made Bathsheba's baby deathly sick. David begged the Lord to spare the child, went without food, and lay all night before the Lord on the bare earth. But on the seventh day the baby died.

I want to look at this story of a man crying out to God to do something for his sick child, but God seemingly closing His ears. I particularly want to look at David's prayer, because *David prayed from a position of faith.* Do not be deluded about this situation. This prayer was extremely difficult for David to say. Remember that Bathsheba's pregnancy was the result of David's forcing himself upon her.

God had already told David what was going to happen. But David prayed nonetheless. Either David was incredibly hardheaded, incredibly callous, incredibly arrogant, incredibly presumptuous — or there may be something we have missed so far. I think it can be put this way. David was defeated, but he was not a failure.

I believe there is a great difference between being defeated and being a failure. A failure is someone who has permanently sunk. A defeated person is a person who has temporarily tripped. Every one of us has had defeats, reversals, disappointments, frustrations, lapses, even serious moral lapses like David's — the kinds of things we would hate for anyone else to know about. But the thing that separates failure from defeat is attitude. It is how we look at and feel about setbacks, and what we do about them, that counts. We are never failures until we believe we are. And what we believe we are is one of the keys to understanding everything that happened in David's life. He always believed in the power of Jehovah. And regardless of how wrong he was sometimes, he believed, and he never let go of that belief. It was this faith that enabled him to launch out and fight a bear that attacked his sheep, or a lion, or a giant, or an army of Philistines, or a king upon his throne, or his own personality, or his own sinfulness. It did not matter what it was — David believed! This is why David was not a failure.

One of the most common reasons for ineffective living is that people make their defeats into permanent failure. Let me tell you about some of my own defeats. As a child I had great feelings of inferiority, and I am by no means free of them now. I never believed in myself, and therefore I found it difficult to believe in God. You see, I believed God had not done a very good job when He created me. That is perhaps one of the worst insults one could ever throw into God's face. "God, if I were You, I would have done a better job." I did not like myself, and I didn't think other people liked me much, either. As I look back on my childhood and teenage years, my low self-esteem stands out clearly in my mind.

I did not have the kinds of gifts and abilities that would make me popular with my peers. As a result, I was often ignored. But I am thankful for those who did not let my defeats become my failure. One of them was a Sunday school teacher. I will never forget or cease to be thankful for him. I felt good when I was around him, because he made me feel I was important.

I have also known defeats in my adult life. One of them almost caused my failure and has left a great scar upon me. It is an experience from which I suppose I will never fully recover. Yet I never cease to wonder at God's grace and the miracles He continues to perform. As a result of my defeated childhood — my low self-image — I can relate to people who have low self-images and feelings of inferiority. I do not pity or ignore them; I understand them. As a result of the defeat in a sad church situation, I was led to one of the most exciting churches in my ministry. I am sure I never would have had such an enriching experience had I not first experienced defeat. I believe it is important to understand that any one of my defeats could well have been my failure. But my faith made the difference.

So it was with David. After his defeats, he was still able to pray — to function — with all the faith in the world. I believe that if there is one roadblock we each have to face, and face continually, it is the fear of failure. We are all afraid of criticism and rejection, of humiliation, of physical or emotional pain. When we are faced with a possibility of failure, we do the natural and easy thing, namely, withdraw, and in many cases, quit praying. We are afraid we will fail even in prayer; afraid we will not be able to cope with God's no; afraid it will make us lose our faith. We realize that if we do not pray we can still believe in prayer. It is when we pray that we make ourselves vulnerable. If we receive a negative answer to our prayers and someone hears about it, how will we be able to hold up our heads? But David prayed even though God told him it was an impossible situation. He prayed as a man who knew defeat, but not failure, and he prayed from a position of faith.

Second, *David prayed from a position of hope*. David was truly a man of hope. When you open your Bible and find verses like Paul's statement in Ephesians 3:20: "Now unto him that is able to do exceeding abundantly above all that we ask or think" (KJV) — it sets you to praying. Verses like Jeremiah 33:3 do likewise: "Call unto me, and I will answer thee, and show thee great and mighty things, which thou knowest not" (KJV). And still more incentive comes from the words of the Sermon on the Mount in Matthew 7:7-8: "Ask, and it shall be given you; seek, and ye shall find; knock, and it shall be opened unto you: For every one that asketh receiveth; and he that seeketh findeth; and to him that knocketh it shall be opened." We petition God in hope, and it was in hope that David prayed. He hoped because he had every reason to hope; God had repeatedly shown him that He was and is the kind of God who will move when asked. Therefore, early in his life, David was able to write the strong words of Psalm 21:1-2: "How the king rejoices in your strength, O Lord! How he exults in your salvation. For you have given him his heart's desire, everything he asks you for!" And David remembered and prayed in hope.

But the same David in the next psalm wrote these words: "My God, my God, why have you forsaken me? Why do you refuse to help me or even to listen to my groans?" (v. 1). And the baby died. David was not alone in seeing his hopes and prayers smashed, however. Jeremiah saw it and told about it in Lamentations 3:44: "You have veiled yourself as with a cloud so that our prayers do not reach through." There was a wall, and when Jeremiah prayed, he thought he did not get any higher than the ceiling. Habakkuk announced right at the beginning of his book: "O Lord, how long must I call for help before you will listen?" (v. 2a). Job knew it, and he cried out in desperation, "I cry to you, O God, but you don't answer me" (Job 30:20a).

And David prayed and the child died. What do you do then? "Is the baby dead?" asked David.

"Yes," they replied, "he is."

Then David got up off the ground, washed himself, brushed his hair, changed his clothes, and went into the tabernacle and worshiped the Lord. What do you do when the child dies? What do you do when your hopes are smashed? You get up, you wash your face, and you get back into life. In a word, like David, our hope needs to go far beyond our prayer.

There is a story about the time the Russian cosmonaut Titov came back from circling the earth nineteen times. Apparently, so the story goes, Premier Nikita Khrushchev went to Titov and asked him if he found God up there. "Yes," said Titov, "I found God up there."

"I always knew He was there," said Khrushchev, "but it's against our policy, so don't tell anybody."

Later Titov was interviewed by a patriarch of the Russian Orthodox Church who asked him the same question. "No," replied Titov, following orders, "I didn't find God up there."

"I always knew he wasn't there," said the patriarch, "but it's against our policy, so don't tell anybody."

For many professing Christians, hope in God is only a false front. It is shallow, precarious, and based on whether God performs according to their likings. If He does not, they stop believing in Him. To them, God is viewed as a kind of fairy godfather. Their prayers go something like this: "Please look after my baby, amuse grandfather, help Willie with his homework, and find a nice, handsome business executive for Muriel to marry. Be interested, God, and do what I ask, and we will all love You and keep right on going to church. But God, watch it! Don't let me down or I'll quit on You."

Never should our hope be pinned on our pet solutions, like Captain Ahab, who thought that if he harpooned the great white whale all his problems would be solved; or like the colonel in the *Bridge Over the River Kwai,* who became so obsessed with the bridge that he thought its completion would neatly solve the problems he and the other British prisoners had at the hands of the Japanese. Healthy hope must always be open to alternatives. When the "child is dead," it is important that we get up off our knees, wash off the tears, and begin again. David's hope went far beyond his prayer. He knew God would answer him, even if He did not grant his request.

Once there was a young man who said, "God, I'll be your man. Send me to India." But God sent him to Burma. "God, please give me a wife with whom I can work." And God gave him a wife; but after a few years she became sick and died. Adoniram Judson prayed for her recovery, but she left him with three small children. Then one by one each of them became sick, and in spite of Judson's prayers, they died, leaving him alone and forsaken. Later, Judson was arrested and thrown into jail for preaching the gospel. While he was in prison he prayed for his release, but it never came.

What does this do to a man who believes in prayer? He lets his hope go far beyond his requests, because he knows God will answer. And God did answer Judson — not with the requests he made, but with Himself. We ask for a gift, and God gives the Giver. Whether prayer changes things is quite beside the point, but one thing is certain: prayer changes *us*. It makes our night become daylight, our winter summer. Our bitterness is sweetened, our grief is healed, and He wipes away our tears. Situations are changed when the people involved in those situations are changed.

Let me give you a little analogy. You may be suffering with a boil on your neck or pneumonia in your left lung. After consultation with your doctor, he may prescribe an antibiotic. And where does he administer it? In the neck or lung? No, he injects it into the fleshy tissue that nature has provided for the purpose. When it passes through hidden channels to the place of the infection, the work is done. We do not know very much about those hidden channels of life. All we see are the infection, the anxiety, the pain, and the suffering. In prayer we offer to God our pain, our anxiety, our "neck" and "lungs," and say, "God, do something"; and God does. Perhaps He does not work directly in the neck or lungs, but He enters the lifestream in a new way, at a greater depth, so that we can get up off our knees and begin to live again.

David prayed from a position of faith and hope. Third, *he prayed from a position of love.* Whenever a man is determined to pray, he must reach for the *hand* of God and not just for the pennies God happens to be holding in His hand. When a person is interested only in the pennies God has, his interest goes no further than the hand itself, because after the person receives the reward, the hand can be pushed away. Such a person views God's hand as only a means to an end. In the First World War, it was said that there were no atheists in the trenches. I wonder how true that was. I wonder if, after the trench situation was over, anyone was still interested in the Hand that had moved to save them.

The story is told about a little boy who got his hand stuck in a vase. This was no ordinary vase. It was a family heirloom and was incredibly valuable. But little boys do not understand such things, and this boy's hand was in it. Try as she could, his mother could not free it. Later his father came home, and the little boy was still walking around with the vase on his hand. After the father tried and failed to get the vase loose, the neighbors came and one by one prescribed a remedy; but no one could get the hand out of the vase. Eventually, in utter grief, they knew that the only thing left for them to do was to smash the vase. When they smashed it, they noticed that the little boy's hand was clenched into a fist, and in the middle of his fist was a penny. He had spied the penny on the bottom of the vase, had taken hold of it, and would not let go.

This is what pained Jesus so much in John 6:26 when He looked around at the people He had just fed and said, "You seek me not because you saw the signs, but because you ate your fill of the loaves" (author's paraphrase). You only see the penny, and that is all you are interested in.

But remember, this is David we are speaking about: David, the one who had great difficulty loving people; David, the one who loved to write psalms, but who wrote only two at the end of his life that proclaimed his love for his God. But now, knowing God had accepted him with all his faults, David began to pray from a position of love. David no longer wore a mask. He knew the kind of person he was and realized that in spite of that, nothing could separate him from the love of God. In a fresh way he understood that God would never turn His back on him, and David finally became secure in that love. No longer was there a need to prove himself. He did not have to go out and do a "Goliath" to win attention and affection. Only now did he feel free to fail without becoming a failure. Only now was he free to hope. David was finally the man God wanted him to be. Yet from this point on, there is no record of any further exploits or colorful adventures. All you read about is a man after God's own heart.

This is why my hero is not a shepherd boy who could tackle a lion or a bear. My David is not the young fellow who could bring a giant crashing to the ground with a slingshot. My hero is not David, the glorious empire builder, the great general, the mighty king. My hero is David the man; he knew defeat yet was not a failure. He had faith, knew the pain of unanswered prayer, yet his hope blossomed. My David is the man who could now finally say, "Now I love you, Lord," and mean it.

Discussion Questions

1. What are some of the reasons that God often does not answer our prayers the way we want Him to?

2. Do you agree that David's praying for God to spare his and Bathsheba's son, even after God had said the child would die, was evidence of great faith rather than presumption? Why or why not? Whose will and glory was David seeking at that point, his own or God's?

3. Do you agree that Christians sometimes do not pray because they are afraid of failure in prayer? Do you ever stop praying for that reason? What can you learn from the life of David to help you overcome that fear?

4. Do you agree that many professing Christians view God only as a fairy godfather, a dispenser of an uninterrupted supply of good things? Do you sometimes think of Him that way? What are some of the spiritual problems that will follow from such a view?

12 How to Live —and Die
2 Samuel 23; 1 Kings 1

David was now old and cold (1 Kings 1:1). To stop his shivering, his servants heaped blankets over him, but to no avail. It was a sad sight — this once dynamic, energetic, and powerful king ending his vigorous life with the shivers. It was a pathetic scene to close what had been a tragic life. David had tasted success, but his success had turned to ashes in his mouth. All through life, his footsteps were dogged by treachery, hatred, rebellion, derision, and murder. Although David made more than his share of foes, he was his own worst enemy. Yet to what extent could he be blamed? How can a man show love to others when he seems to have received so little of it himself? Once, when he did open his heart's door a crack and let a little love seep through, his heart was trampled over and broken. And now the icy fingers of death had him in their grip.

What was to become of his kingdom? How long would it last with its architect removed? A lesser man could easily have wailed, "I'm tired, I'm weak, I'm old, and I'm cold. Let them do what they like with my kingdom. They can take all I've got for all I care." But David had never lived that way, and he had no intention of dying that way. Here, then, is a story for those who think that life has shortchanged them. It is a story for those who think that too much has been demanded of them. It is particularly a story for those who have reached the point of saying, "I can't go on. I'm at the end of my rope. Everyone is against me. I feel I'm about to crack up."

In this concluding chapter on the life of David, we will consider three key words that to me sum up David's life and, indeed, David's death. The first of these words is *power*. At this point, let me introduce you to David's eldest living son, Adonijah. Adonijah's two older brothers had been murdered, so he was left to occupy the center stage. Like many another power-hungry prince, Adonijah began to speculate about who would be the next king. No precedent had yet been set, and no heir apparent had yet been named. None of King Saul's sons had succeeded him to the throne, so there was no reason to assume that any of David's sons should automatically become king. But Adonijah thought that he alone was the man to rule. And why should he wait for his old, cold father to die? Why should he wait for his younger brothers to elbow their way into leadership?

So Adonijah laid his plans for usurping his father's throne, and his campaign was subtle. He knew that he had to have influential supporters, and he got them. First, he convinced David's right-hand man and commander-in-chief, Joab, to support his bid. So he had a general on his side. Now, who else? Well, he knew he should make his campaign religious and respectable, so he also needed a priest. The man Adonijah chose was Abiathar, another of David's trusted advisers.

Adonijah then had all the influence he thought he needed, on the one hand a great general and on the other hand a revered priest. He was ready to proclaim himself king in place of his old and cold father. "So he hired chariots and drivers and recruited fifty men to run down the streets before him as royal footmen" (1 Kings 1:5). And a great celebration with a host of invited dignitaries was held to announce his coronation.

Let me digress for a moment and admit that I am puzzled. What kind of man *was* David? What kind of father could produce such a family of rebellious and treacherous sons? What kind of king would surround himself with such scheming and plotting people as Joab and Abiathar? And speaking of Joab and Abiathar, were they so fickle that they could drop David lightly after having been trusted by him for fifty years, turning their affections to someone as blatantly unsuitable as Adonijah?

Now as Adonijah, Joab, and Abiathar made their plans, they forgot that David knew a great deal about power, specifically, the power of the Holy Spirit. We have seen in previous chapters the many times and many ways in which God's power enabled David to mature and overcome.

Through the centuries, God has called many like David and empowered them for His service. But as you read the biographies of such men and discover their strange idiosyncrasies and character flaws, you wonder why God chose them. Yet in spite of their flaws and weaknesses, God was somehow honored as He displayed His power through them; and all we can say is that God's ways are not our ways, and His thoughts are not our thoughts.

Isn't this what grace is all about? There is nothing commendable about any of us until Jesus Christ puts His hand upon us and says, "I make you Mine." It is not because we are nice people that God says, "I would like to have you in My service." It is not because we have sweet and gentle personalities that God says, "Ah, what would I do without you? You are the answer to My prayer." In ourselves we may be repulsive, foul, selfish, greedy, corrupt, and treacherous, but none of this stops God. He still stoops down, however deep in the mud we are, and picks us up.

When we come to Him through faith in His Son, Jesus Christ, He picks us up with all our personal ugliness, holds us to Himself, and says, "I forgive you as though none of this were true of you. I take you to the cross of My Son, Jesus Christ, and there I transfer your guilt to Him and His purity to you." Then into these same previously warped individuals God puts His power, His Holy Spirit, and sends us out — the most unlikely ambassadors to do His work in the world. What a fantastic God we have! Others may despise us, but not God.

Yes, David may have known little about love, joy, and peace in his life, but he did know a great deal about power. And somehow, Abiathar and Joab overlooked that fact. They, above all of David's aides, should have borne it in mind, because they had seen the Spirit at work in and through David — this Spirit whose power filled and characterized David's life and death.

There is a second key word in the summation of David's personality, *commitment*. To illustrate the significance of this word in David's life, let's take another look at Adonijah's banquet, at that point in full swing. The stage seemed to be set. The supporters were ecstatic. The way seemed clear for Adonijah to take the throne. But he had made one fatal blunder. He had overlooked Nathan, and Nathan had an uncanny knack of finding things out. Nearly thirty years earlier, Nathan had uncovered David's guilty secret about Bathsheba and confronted him with it. Now he uncovered Adonijah's plot.

Nathan was a formidable foe. He knew that David intended for Solomon to succeed him. So Nathan moved fast. Realizing that David must always be approached indirectly, Nathan enlisted the aid of the beautiful Bathsheba to prepare the king for Nathan's arrival. Bathsheba, always ready to advance the cause of her own son, Solomon, recounted to David Adonijah's campaign tactics. Before she

finished her speech, Nathan entered and confirmed the
report — but with a slight twist so there would be no sign of
collaboration.

And Nathan went in and bowed low before the king.
Then he said, "Your Majesty, have you announced that
Adonijah would succeed you as king? This very day he
has gone and offered a sacrifice of many bulls, sheep,
and fattened calves. He invited all your sons, Joab the
commander of your army, and Abiathar the priest, and
right now they are feasting with him and shouting,
'Long live King Adonijah!'" [1 Kings 1:23-25, TEV].

Now the key to grasping this narrative is to watch the
impact this news had on David. He was old and he was
cold, but was he finished? Had the burden of life quenched
the final spark of energy? Had all the pain and intrigue and
sorrow reduced David to a nobody? True, his outward form
was pathetic. But down in the depths of David's heart still
glowed the same spark that had been there a lifetime. And
this was just the situation to fan that spark into a blaze
again. This is an extremely important narrative, for it allows
the true David to emerge. Further, it illustrates a vital life
principle that is enacted in your experience and mine far
more frequently than we realize.

In my seminary's library hung a motto that came from
Bishop Taylor Smith, a great British preacher. It had four
words on it: "As now, so then." During my seminary days,
it did not seem to make much sense to me. In fact, I thought
it was a peculiar motto to hang in a seminary library. But as I
grew older and more experienced, I grew to see the great
wisdom in the motto. If I capitulate now, the chances of my
capitulating tomorrow are that much greater, and so are
they greater next week, next month, and next year. If I fail
to meet the challenge of an opportunity today, at this moment, I will not be prepared to meet other challenges that
present themselves in the future. I will have lost my training chances.

We begin fashioning our reaction to life in childhood. If I began by being self-indulgent, lazy, and selfish, so I will continue through adulthood. There will be no magic wand waved over me to make me suddenly a different personality. The seeds I sow in my life today will be reaped year after year after year. As I am now (no set of circumstances is going to alter me), so I will be then.

It is the same with our Christian life. If I commit my life to Jesus Christ now, without reservation, and learn early to yield to His direction and submit to His truth, then when demands are placed upon me, that commitment will hold me. When I yield to Christ and obey His laws, I become strong for anything life may throw at me. Then, when I become too old to keep warm, miracles will happen. The impossible will be achieved.

Do you remember what happened to David in 2 Samuel 24? He wanted to make a sacrifice at a particular place and at a particular time. The ideal spot was at the top of Mount Moriah, close to what was then his capital city, Jerusalem. David went to see Araunah, who owned a threshing floor at the top of Mount Moriah, and asked to buy it.

"Why have you come?" Araunah asked.

And David replied, "To buy your threshing floor, so that I can build an altar to the Lord, and he will stop the plague."

"Use anything you like," Araunah told the king. "Here are oxen for the burnt offering, and you can use the threshing instruments and ox yokes for wood to build a fire on the altar. I will give it all to you, and may the Lord God accept your sacrifice."

But the king said to Araunah, "No, I will not have it as a gift. I will buy it, for I don't want to offer to the Lord my God burnt offerings that have cost me nothing" [vv. 21-24].

This was the commitment that burned in David's heart. "My devotion to God has got to cost me something. I am

not willing to make a token offering to Him. My commitment is such that it has got to hurt." How fitting that David
should choose Mount Moriah for such a sacrifice, because
Moriah is the area in which Abraham had been before him
to offer up *his* greatest and best offering, his son Isaac.

I trust that in your spiritual experience God has led you
up the mountain of Calvary, where you have found par-
don, peace, and forgiveness for your sin. That is a moun-
tain-top experience! But have you ever walked up Mount
Moriah? Have you ever taken a lonely pilgrimage up there
and let Christ go with you to the place of opportunity?
David did, and that kind of commitment is the secret to
David's life and death.

As now, so then. And because he lived that way, he could
die that way. Total commitment to God and His plan had
become the pattern engraved upon his life. When everything seems lost, the miracles happen. In 1 Kings 1:32-35,
we see this weak, frozen, shriveled old king accept the
challenge.

"Call Zadok the priest," the king ordered, "and Nathan
the prophet, and Benaiah." When they arrived, he said
to them, "Take Solomon and my officers to Gihon. Solomon is to ride on my personal mule, and Zadok the
priest and Nathan the prophet are to anoint him there as
king of Israel. Then blow the trumpets and shout, 'Long
live King Solomon!' When you bring him back here,
place him upon my throne as the new king; for I have
appointed him king of Israel and Judah."

A few minutes before, David had been lying there, shivering. Now he was snapping out orders right and left. Why?
Because the whole course of his life had been set this way —
commitment, complete commitment.

There is a third and final word characterizing David's life
that is significant — power, commitment, and now *trust*.
Just think about this for a moment. Think about David's

apparently unpromising home, about the struggles, the fights and feuds, the tragedy of his own home and family, the power and might, the intrigue and plots, the adultery and murder. But think most of all about David and God. David knew God very well, but God knew David much better. What fascinates me is how the two of them got together. David was a man who complained bitterly, but he also gave great praise to God. He was a man who killed and destroyed, but he was also a man who sometimes did the right thing; and this is why David's story makes sense.

It is the story of any one of us. It is my story; it is your story. Sometimes we are with the wicked, and sometimes we are with the righteous. But the secret of what happened to David is simply this: everything that took place in his life was God-related. This alone is the reason David is called "a man after God's own heart." Whether it was success or failure, goodness or badness; whether it was righteousness or evil, the fine points of his character or the foul ones — everything was seen in his relationship to God. This complete God-centeredness, or trust, is what I want. I do not want David's failures, successes, or power. I certainly do not want his home life. No, it is David's God I want. I want to find Him, know Him, and love Him. As I look at David's story, I realize that it was not David who found God. Rather, God found David. God said to Samuel, "I have provided a king for myself." Therefore, to really know David we have to see David as he always was in his heart — not a king, but a shepherd. He was not a man who could relate to people. He was a man who could relate to sheep, trusting creatures who are totally dependent on their shepherd.

We find that God had His hand upon David, not because David was a nice boy — he was never a nice boy — but because he and God had something special between them. David never saw God as a father (fathers were not very high on David's esteem list) or as a friend (friends proved too fickle). Rather, David saw God as a Shepherd. He could understand that kind of relationship. And he did not see himself as a son or even as a subject of the King. He saw himself as a sheep. David knew sheep. He knew that sheep do nothing to earn the right to be loved and protected. All they have to do is to be themselves and trust the shepherd.

So I look deep into the eyes of David as he sits, perhaps on some grassy Judean hillside, surrounded by the bleating of sheep, drinking from the clear, cool water of a gentle stream, and I hear him say softly, "The Lord is my Shepherd."

"Yes, David, that's fine. But today the sun is shining, God is in His heaven, and all's right with the world. You can talk about green pastures and cool water now. But what about those times when you will find yourself confused and uncertain, when you take the law into your own hands, and you make the wrong decisions and wrong choices? What about those times when you will take the wrong path?"

"Then He will restore me to the right path. Then He will lead me in the paths of righteousness for His name's sake!"

"Yes, David, but life is rough. What about when sorrow comes? When your baby dies, how will you handle grief? When your only friend is killed in battle, how will you cope? When you encounter murder and incest in your own family, what will you do? When your rebellious son is hung by his hair and murdered, where will your Shepherd be then, David?"

"Yea, though I walk through the valley of the shadow of death, I will fear no evil. Why not? Because He, my Shepherd, is with me!"

"But, David, can you, only a little sheep, hold out when you're hunted like an animal, chased through the desert, and forced to hide in caves for fear of your life? How long do you think you will last when your throat is parched with thirst and those pangs of hunger grip you?"

"Thou preparest a table before me in the presence of mine enemies. My cup runneth over!"

"But David, what right have you, of all people, to expect God to bless you? You, who have taken God's laws and torn them to shreds; you, who have taken His commandments and trodden them underfoot; you, who have failed as a husband, a father, and a friend; you, who stand guilty and condemned by your own conscience. David, how can you expect God to be good to you?"

"Surely *goodness* and *mercy* shall follow me all the days of my life — that is my unshakable conviction. And I will dwell in the house of the Lord *forever!*"

"David, will you write that down for me? I need to know that. And will you write it down for the countless broken, hopeless people who know what it's like to fail? And will you write it down for those who have messed up their marriages, as you did, and fouled up their children's lives, as you did? And will you write it down for those who have never really known love, or joy, or peace? David, please, will you write it down for *me?*"

"The Lord is my Shepherd. . . ."

Discussion Questions

1. Given that David's response to Adonijah's plot showed there was still some energy and determination in him, how did David end up as a cold, worn-out old man, huddling under a pile of blankets? Compare David at the end of his life to Moses at the end of his (Deut. 34:7).

2. What kind of men do you think Joab and Abiathar were? What qualities had made them trusted advisers of David? Why did they desert him for Adonijah? What lessons are there from their lives for leaders today?

3. Summarize in your own words, in twenty-five words or less, what made David "a man after God's own heart."

4. Having looked at David in all his successes and failures, which of his characteristics would you most like to emulate? Why? Which would you most like to avoid? Why?